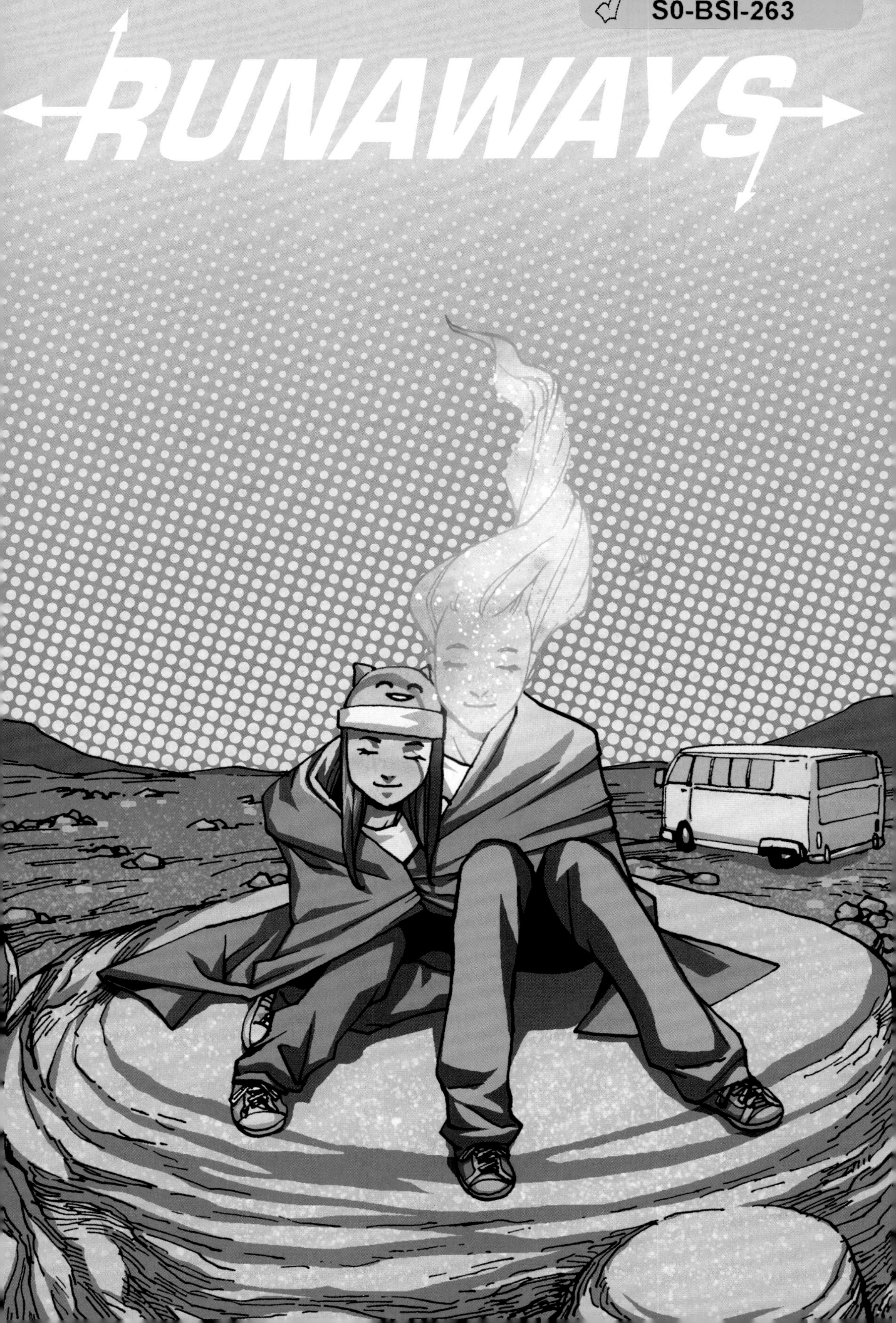
RUNAWAYS

RUNAWAYS

ROCK ZOMBIES

RUNAWAYS #7-9
WRITER: **TERRY MOORE**
PENCILS: **TAKESHI MIYAZAWA**
INKS: **TAKESHI MIYAZAWA** (#7-9), **NORMAN LEE** (#8),
   CRAIG YEUNG (#8) & **ROLAND PARIS** (#9)

RUNAWAYS #10
   "MOLLIFEST DESTINY"
   WRITER: **CHRISTOPHER YOST**
   ARTIST: **SARA PICHELLI**
   "TRUTH OR DARE"
   WRITER: **JAMES ASMUS**
   ARTIST: **EMMA RIOS**

COLORS: **CHRISTINA STRAIN**
LETTERS: **VC's JOE CARAMAGNA**
COVER ART: **HUMBERTO RAMOS** & **CHRISTINA STRAIN**
EDITORS: **NICK LOWE** & **DANIEL KETCHUM**

RUNAWAYS CREATED BY **BRIAN K. VAUGHAN** & **ADRIAN ALPHONA**

RUNAWAYS VOL. 10: ROCK ZOMBIES. Contains material originally published in magazine form as RUNAWAYS #7-10. Second edition. First printing 2018. ISBN 978-1-302-90911-6. Published by MARVEL WORLDWIDE, INC., a subsidiary of MARVEL ENTERTAINMENT, LLC. OFFICE OF PUBLICATION: 135 West 50th Street, New York, NY 10020. Copyright © 2018 MARVEL No similarity between any of the names, characters, persons, and/or institutions in this magazine with those of any living or dead person or institution is intended, and any such similarity which may exist is purely coincidental. **Printed in Canada.** DAN BUCKLEY, President, Marvel Entertainment; JOE QUESADA, Chief Creative Officer; TOM BREVOORT, SVP of Publishing; DAVID BOGART, SVP of Business Affairs & Operations, Publishing & Partnership; DAVID GABRIEL, SVP of Sales & Marketing, Publishing; JEFF YOUNGQUIST, VP of Production & Special Projects; DAN CARR, Executive Director of Publishing Technology; ALEX MORALES, Director of Publishing Operations; SUSAN CRESPI, Production Manager; STAN LEE, Chairman Emeritus. For information regarding advertising in Marvel Comics or on Marvel.com, please contact Vit DeBellis, Custom Solutions & Integrated Advertising Manager, at vdebellis@marvel.com. For Marvel subscription inquiries, please call 888-511-5480. **Manufactured between 2/23/2018 and 3/27/2018 by SOLISCO PRINTERS, SCOTT, QC, CANADA.**

10 9 8 7 6 5 4 3 2 1

COLLECTION EDITOR: **JENNIFER GRÜNWALD**
ASSISTANT EDITOR: **CAITLIN O'CONNELL**
ASSOCIATE MANAGING EDITOR: **KATERI WOODY**
EDITOR, SPECIAL PROJECTS: **MARK D. BEAZLEY**
VP PRODUCTION & SPECIAL PROJECTS: **JEFF YOUNGQUIST**
SVP PRINT, SALES & MARKETING: **DAVID GABRIEL**

EDITOR IN CHIEF: **C.B. CEBULSKI**
CHIEF CREATIVE OFFICER: **JOE QUESADA**
PRESIDENT: **DAN BUCKLEY**
EXECUTIVE PRODUCER: **ALAN FINE**

PREVIOUSLY:

AT SOME POINT IN THEIR LIVES, ALL KIDS THINK THAT THEIR PARENTS ARE EVIL. FOR MOLLY HAYES AND HER FRIENDS, THIS IS ESPECIALLY TRUE.

ONE NIGHT, MOLLY AND HER FRIENDS DISCOVERED THAT THEIR PARENTS WERE A GROUP OF SUPER-POWERED CRIME BOSSES WHO CALLED THEMSELVES "THE PRIDE." USING TECHNOLOGY AND RESOURCES STOLEN FROM THEIR PARENTS, THE TEENAGERS WERE ABLE TO STOP THE PRIDE AND BREAK THEIR CRIMINAL HOLD ON LOS ANGELES. BUT THEY'VE BEEN ON THE RUN ON EVER SINCE.

ATTACKED BY A CREW OF MAJESDANIAN SOLDIERS INTENT ON CAPTURING THE RUNAWAYS' KAROLINA DEAN — WHOM THEY HOLD RESPONSIBLE FOR THE DESTRUCTION OF THEIR HOME PLANET — THE RUNAWAYS FIGHT BACK AND DO EVERYTHING THEY CAN TO ESCAPE. BUT WHEN THEY REALIZE THAT THIS IS A FIGHT THEY WON'T BE ABLE TO WIN, THE SHAPE-SHIFTING XAVIN TAKES KAROLINA'S PLACE AND WILLINGLY AGREES TO GO WITH THE MAJESDANIANS, LEAVING HER FELLOW RUNAWAYS BEHIND.

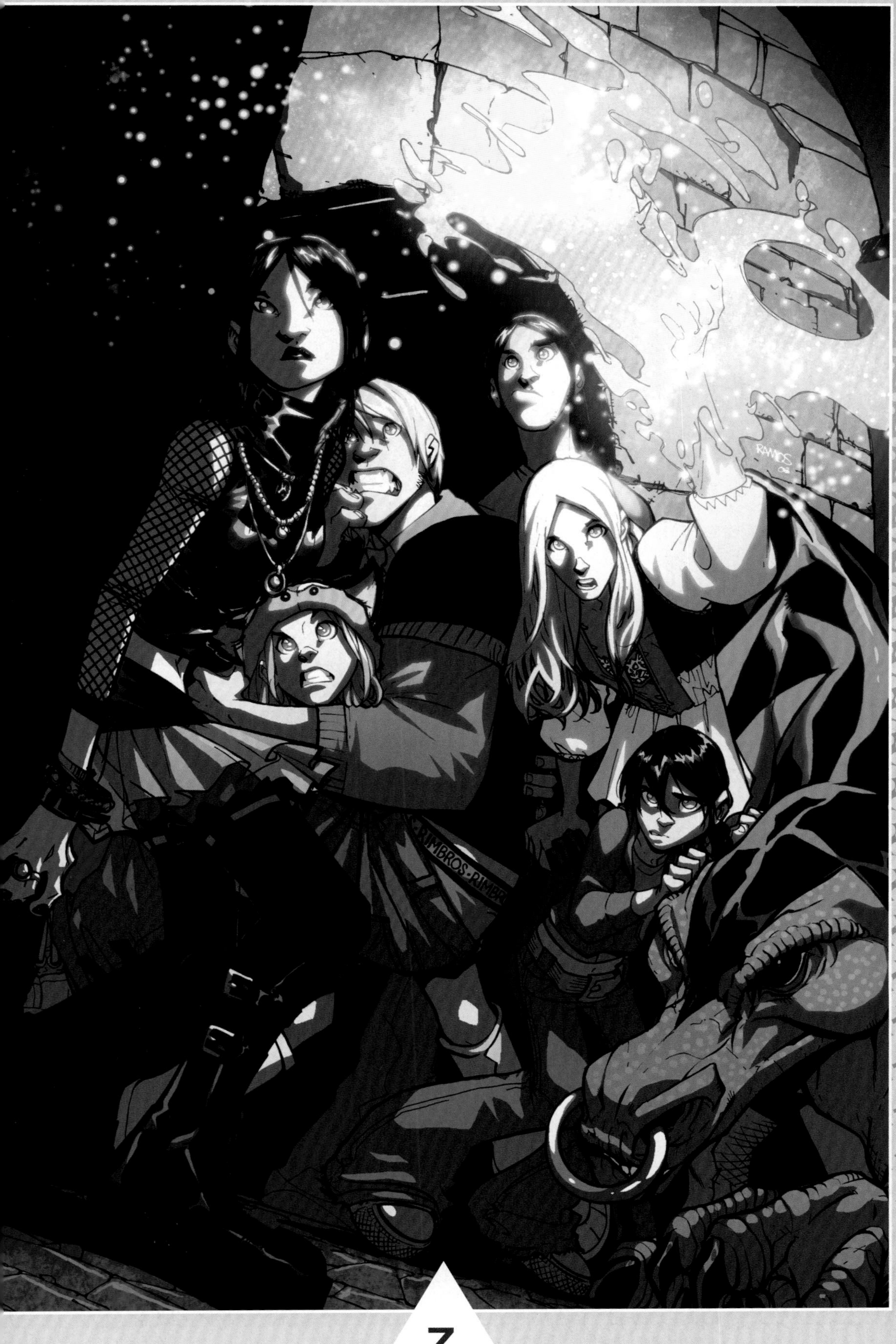
RAMOS 08
RIMBROS·RIMBROS·RIMBRO

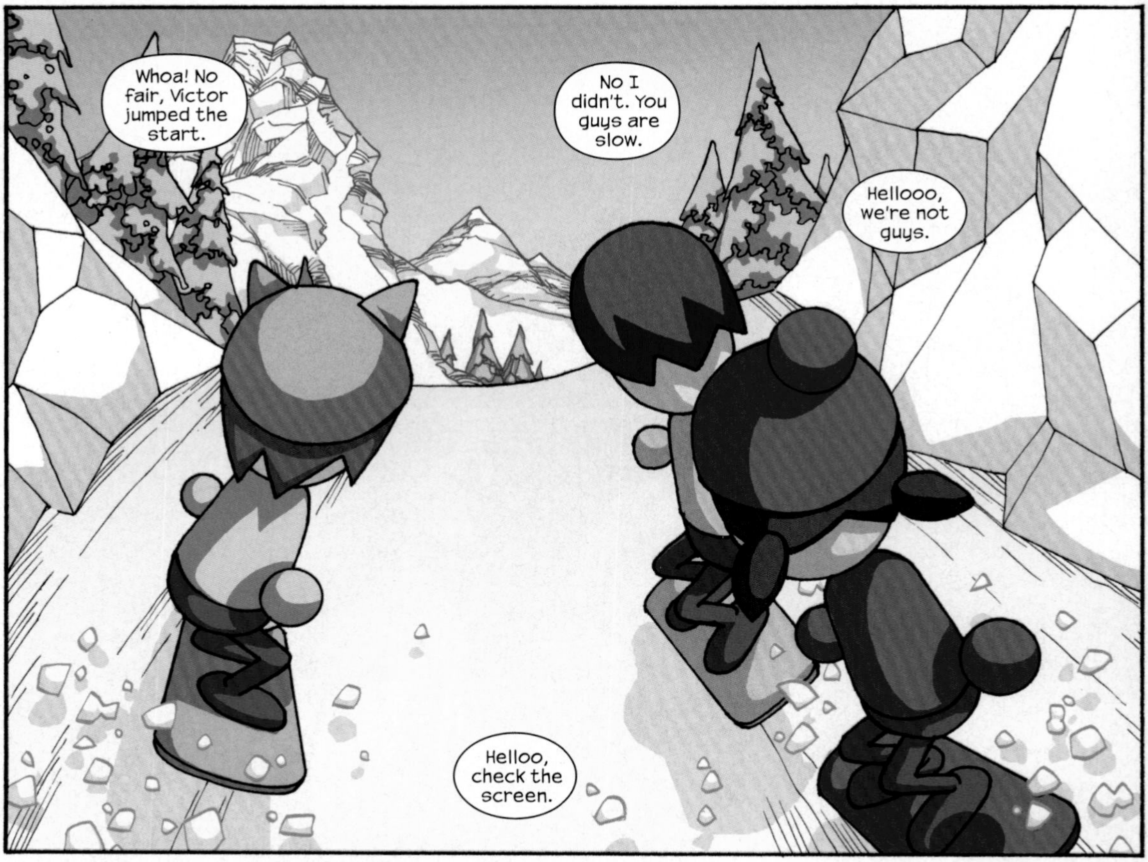
Whoa! No fair, Victor jumped the start.
No I didn't. You guys are slow.
Hellooo, we're not guys.
Helloo, check the screen.

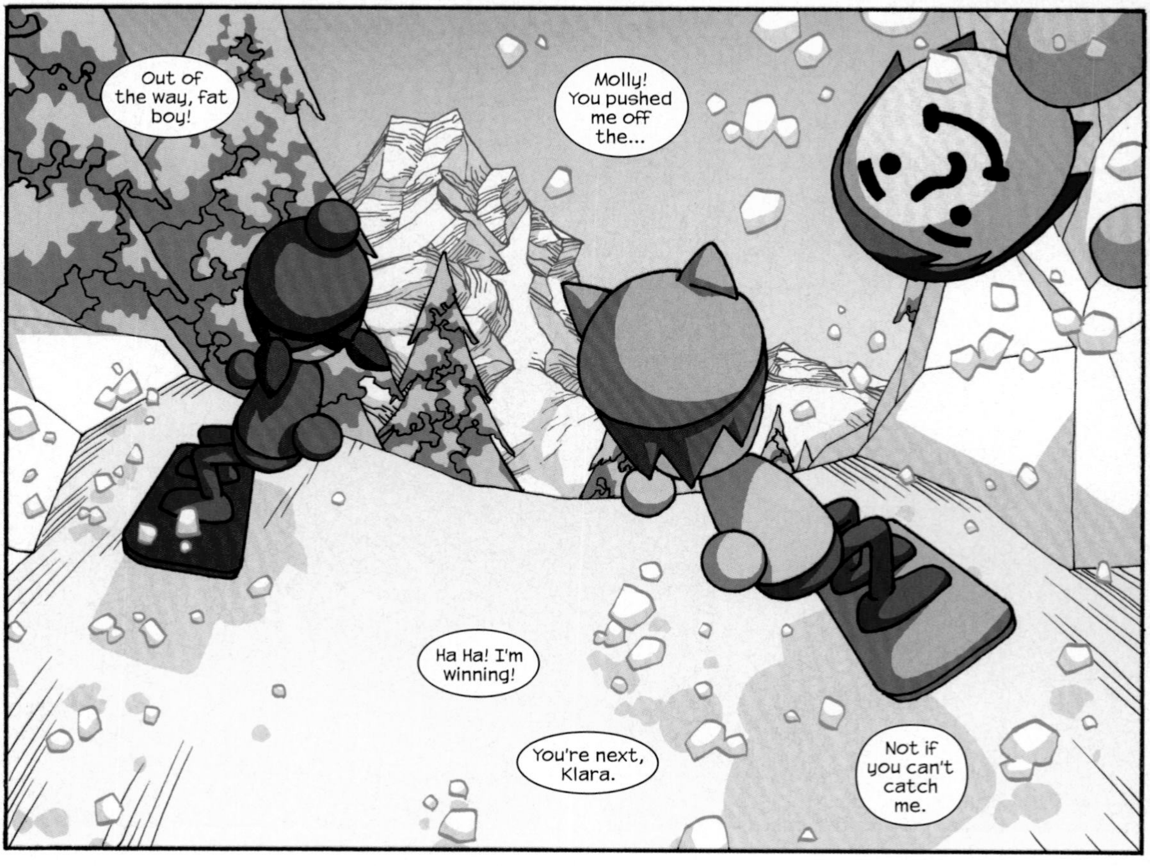
Out of the way, fat boy!
Molly! You pushed me off the...
Ha Ha! I'm winning!
You're next, Klara.
Not if you can't catch me.

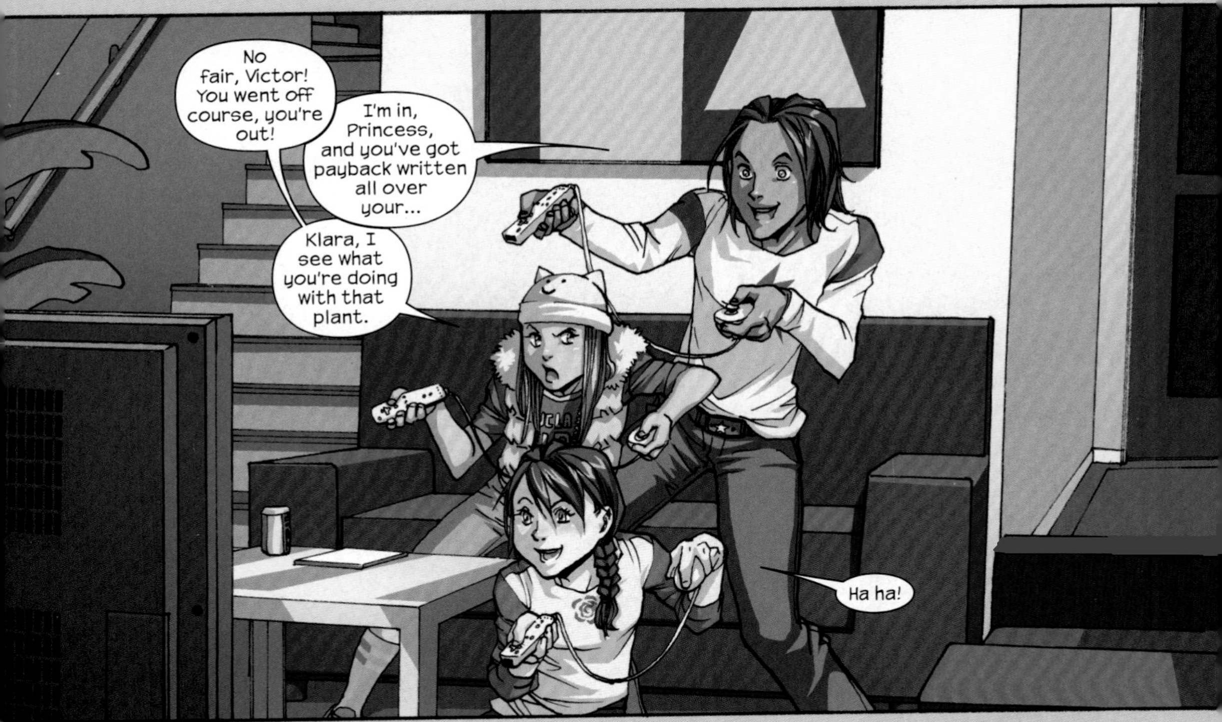
No fair, Victor! You went off course, you're out!
I'm in, Princess, and you've got payback written all over your...
Klara, I see what you're doing with that plant.
Ha ha!

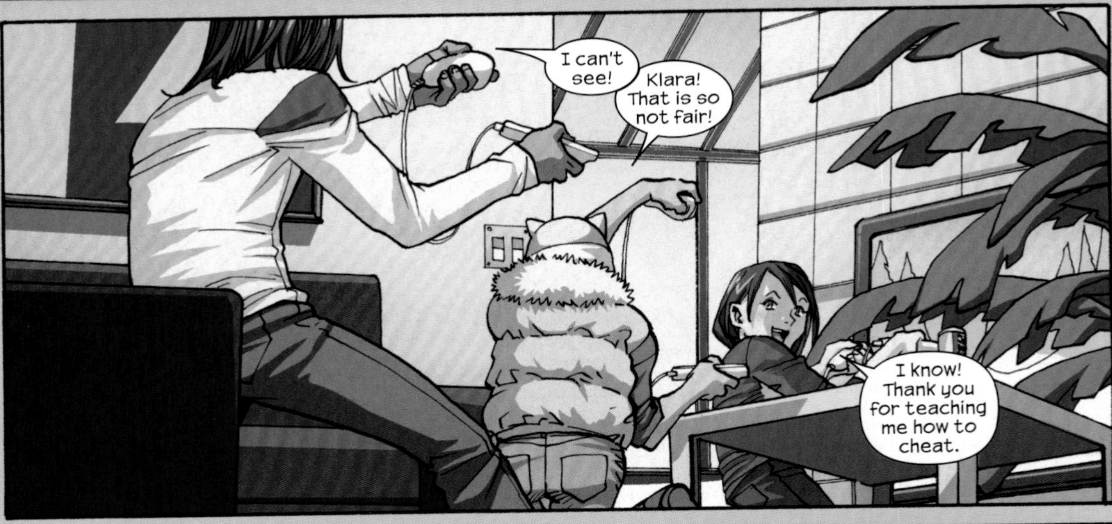
I can't see!
Klara! That is so not fair!
I know! Thank you for teaching me how to cheat.

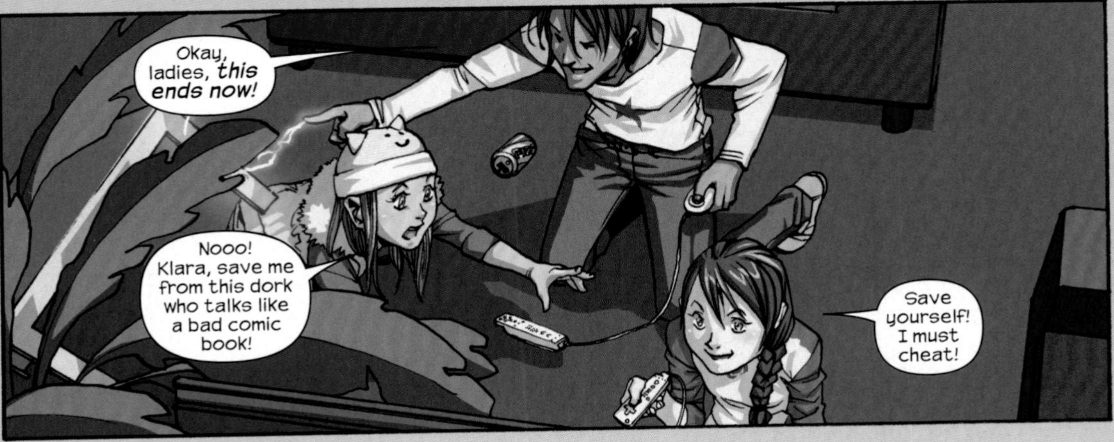
Okay, ladies, *this ends now!*
Nooo! Klara, save me from this dork who talks like a bad comic book!
Save yourself! I must cheat!

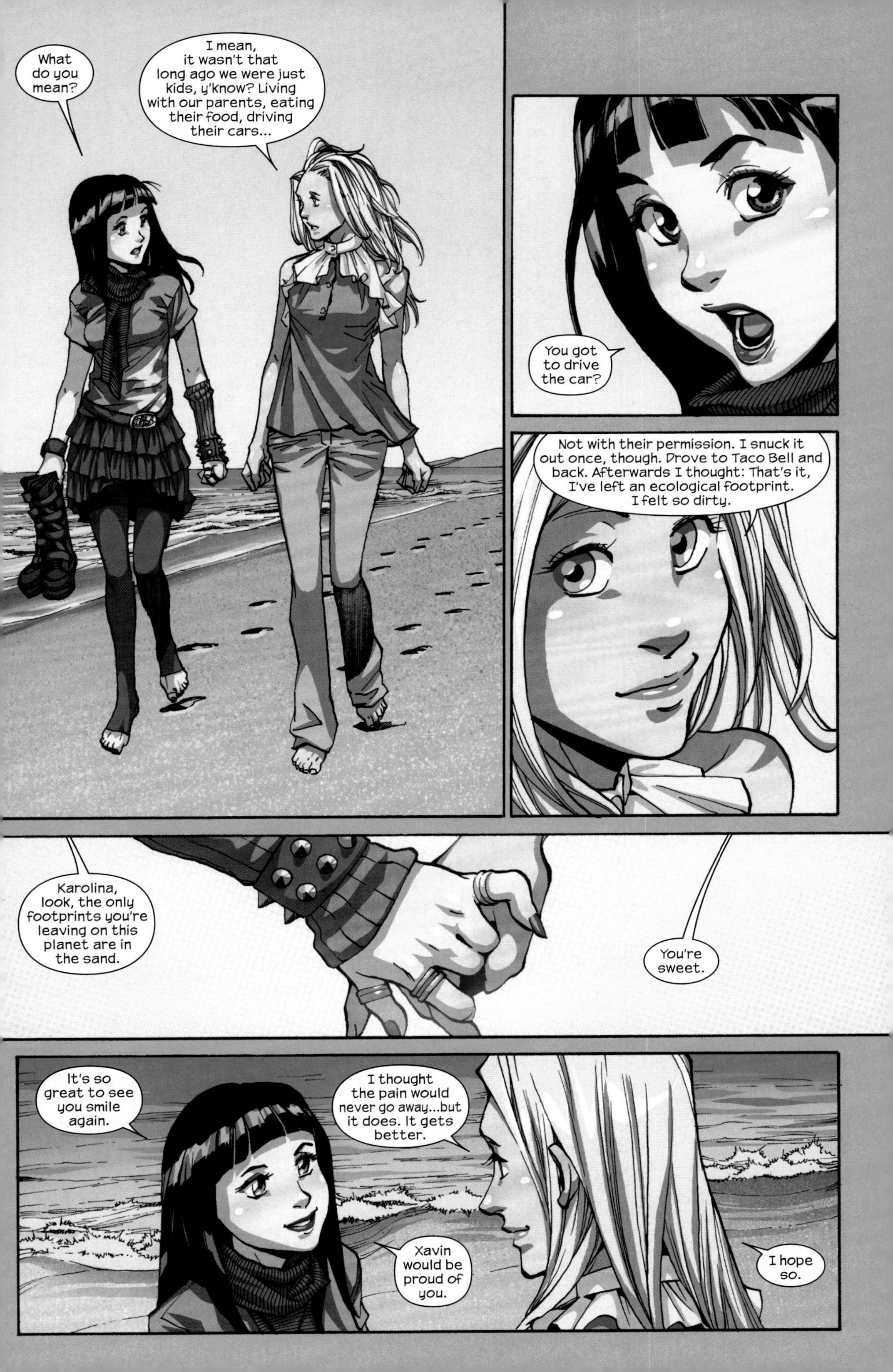
What do you mean?
I mean, it wasn't that long ago we were just kids, y'know? Living with our parents, eating their food, driving their cars...
You got to drive the car?
Not with their permission. I snuck it out once, though. Drove to Taco Bell and back. Afterwards I thought: That's it, I've left an ecological footprint. I felt so dirty.
Karolina, look, the only footprints you're leaving on this planet are in the sand.
You're sweet.
It's so great to see you smile again.
I thought the pain would never go away...but it does. It gets better.
Xavin would be proud of you.
I hope so.

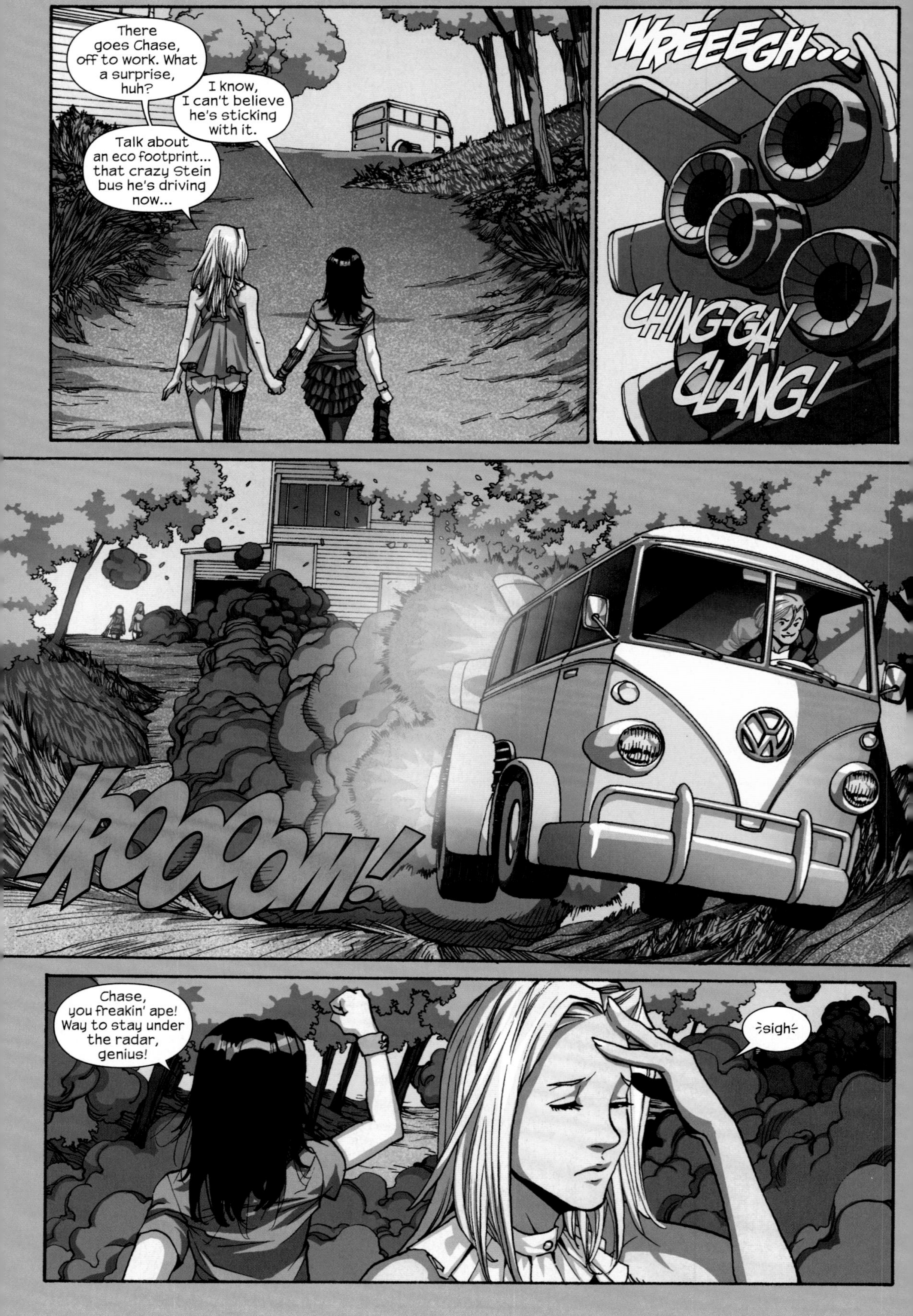
There goes Chase, off to work. What a surprise, huh?
I know, I can't believe he's sticking with it.
Talk about an eco footprint... that crazy Stein bus he's driving now...
WREEEGH...
CHING-GA!
CLANG!
VROOOOM!
Chase, you freakin' ape! Way to stay under the radar, genius!
sigh

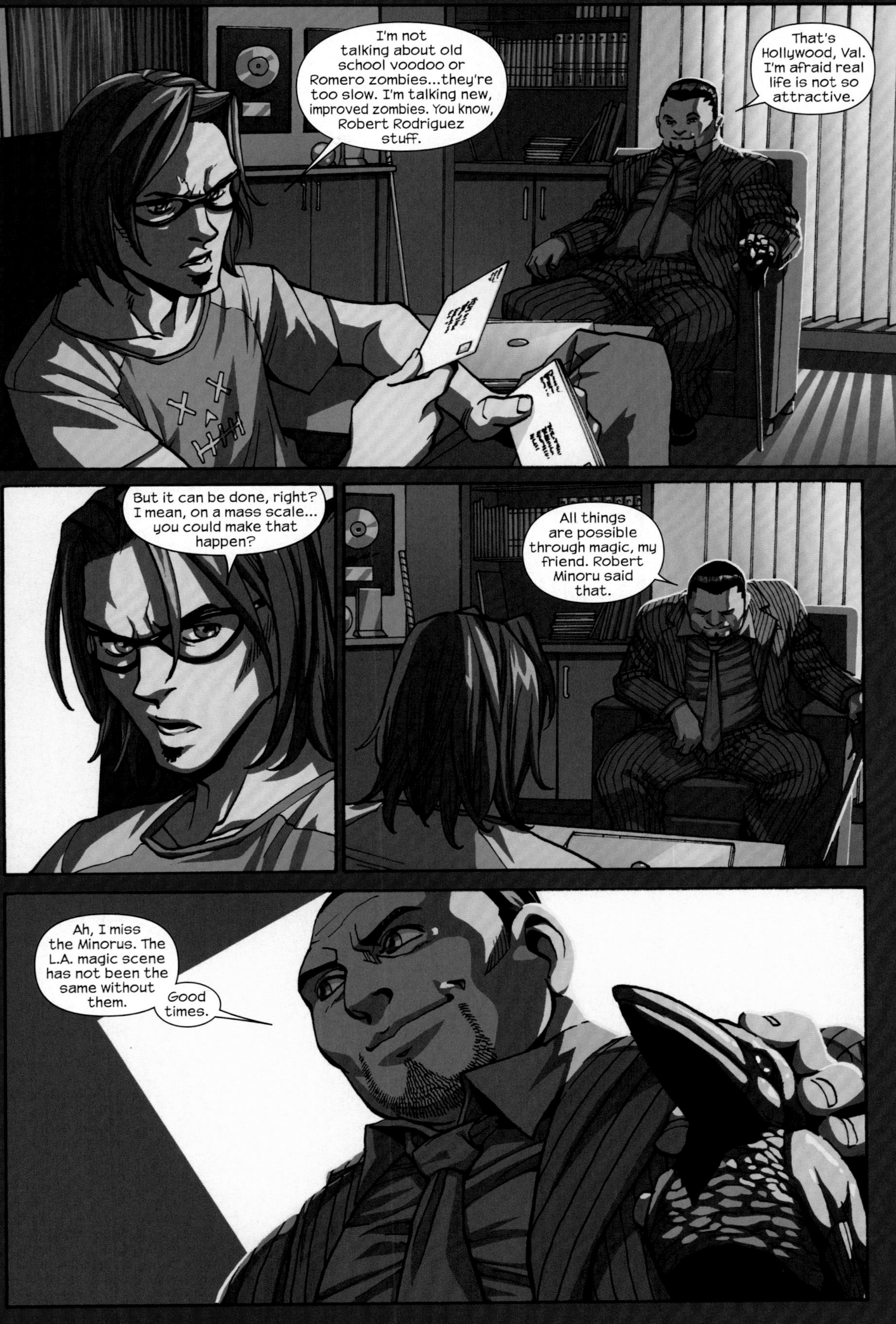

I'm not talking about old school voodoo or Romero zombies...they're too slow. I'm talking new, improved zombies. You know, Robert Rodriguez stuff.
That's Hollywood, Val. I'm afraid real life is not so attractive.
But it can be done, right? I mean, on a mass scale... you could make that happen?
All things are possible through magic, my friend. Robert Minoru said that.
Ah, I miss the Minorus. The L.A. magic scene has not been the same without them.
Good times.

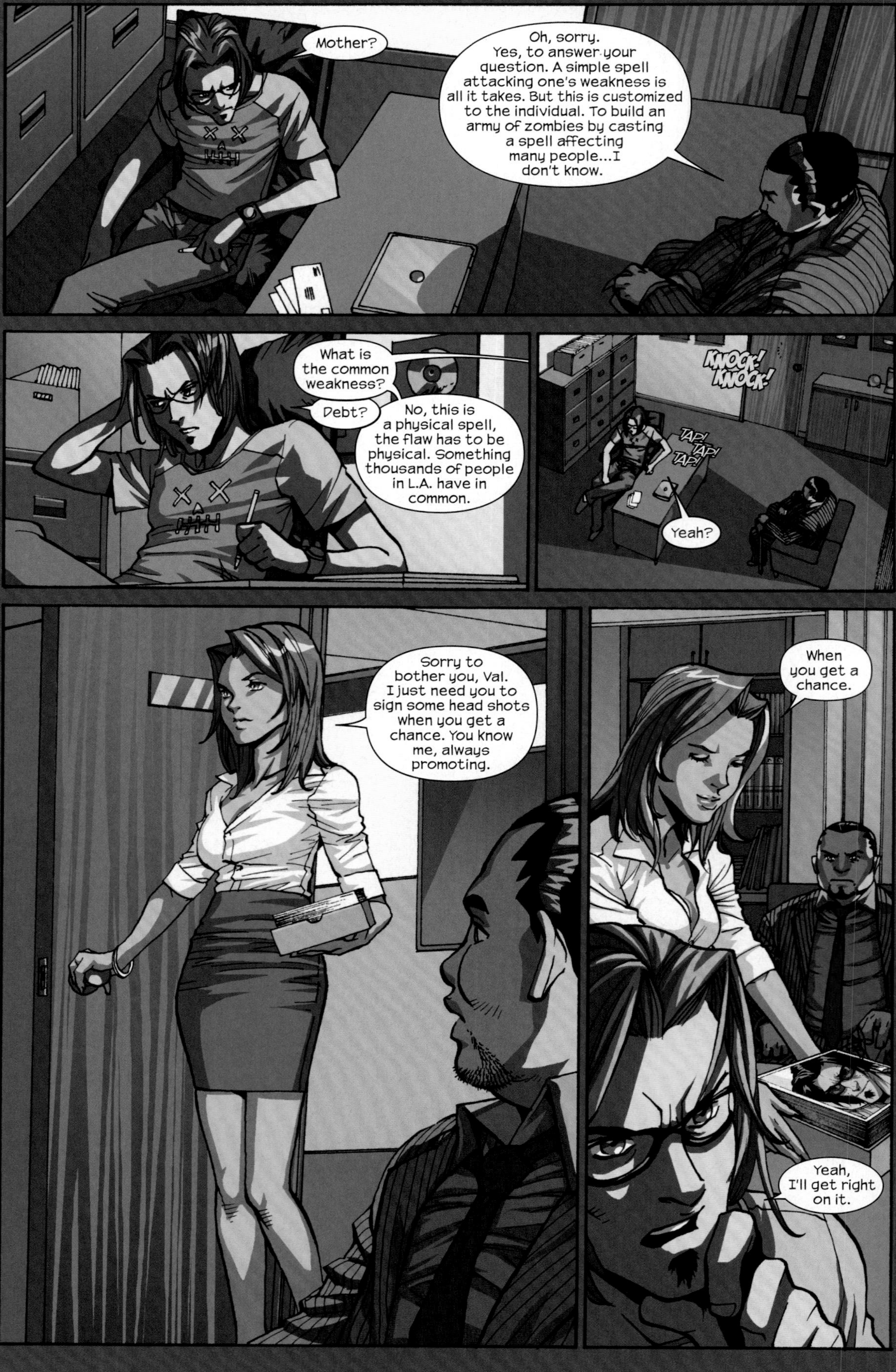
Mother?
Oh, sorry. Yes, to answer your question. A simple spell attacking one's weakness is all it takes. But this is customized to the individual. To build an army of zombies by casting a spell affecting many people...I don't know.
What is the common weakness?
Debt?
No, this is a physical spell, the flaw has to be physical. Something thousands of people in L.A. have in common.
KNOCK! KNOCK!
TAP! TAP! TAP!
Yeah?
Sorry to bother you, Val. I just need you to sign some head shots when you get a chance. You know me, always promoting.
When you get a chance.
Yeah, I'll get right on it.

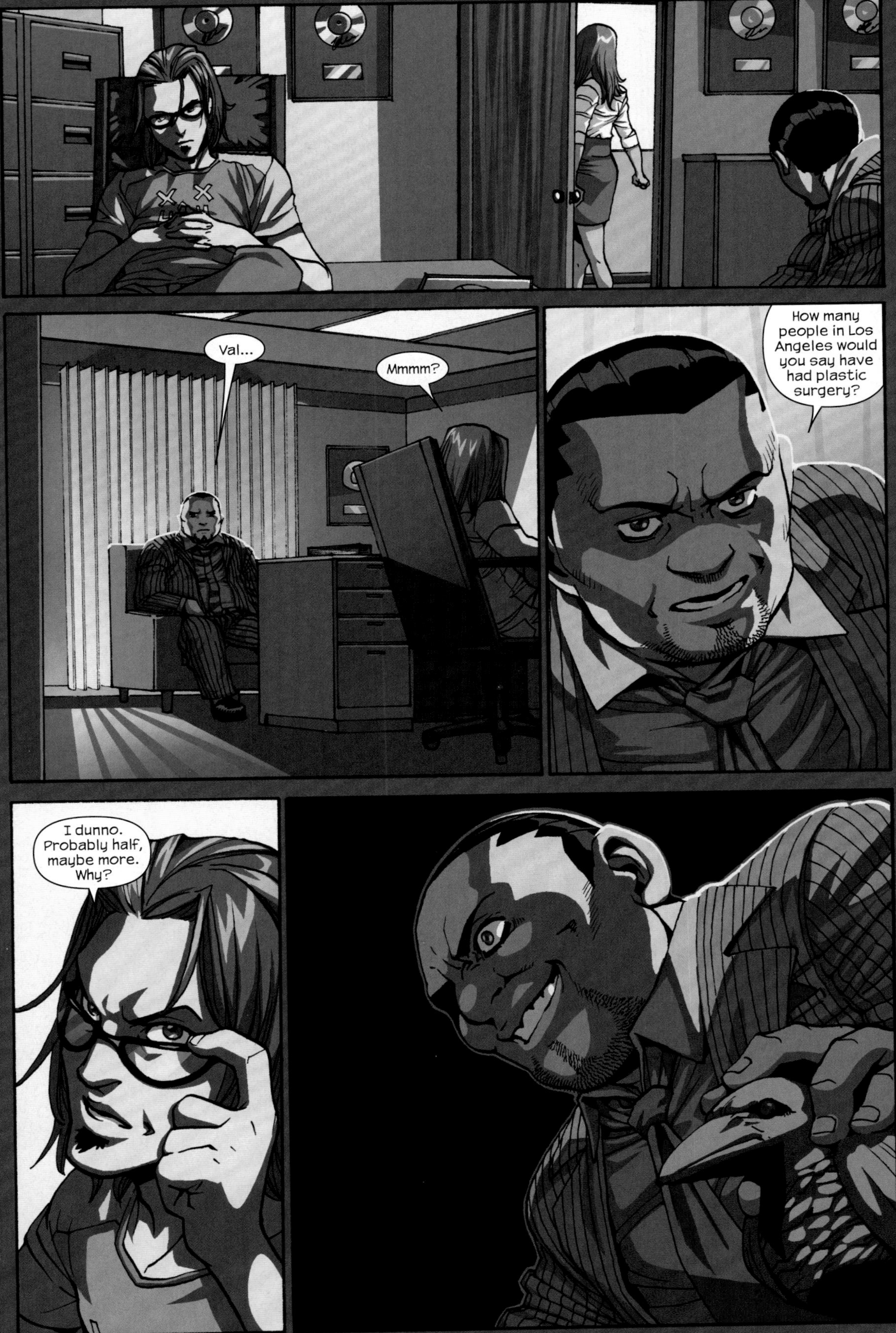
Val...
Mmmm?
How many people in Los Angeles would you say have had plastic surgery?
I dunno. Probably half, maybe more. Why?

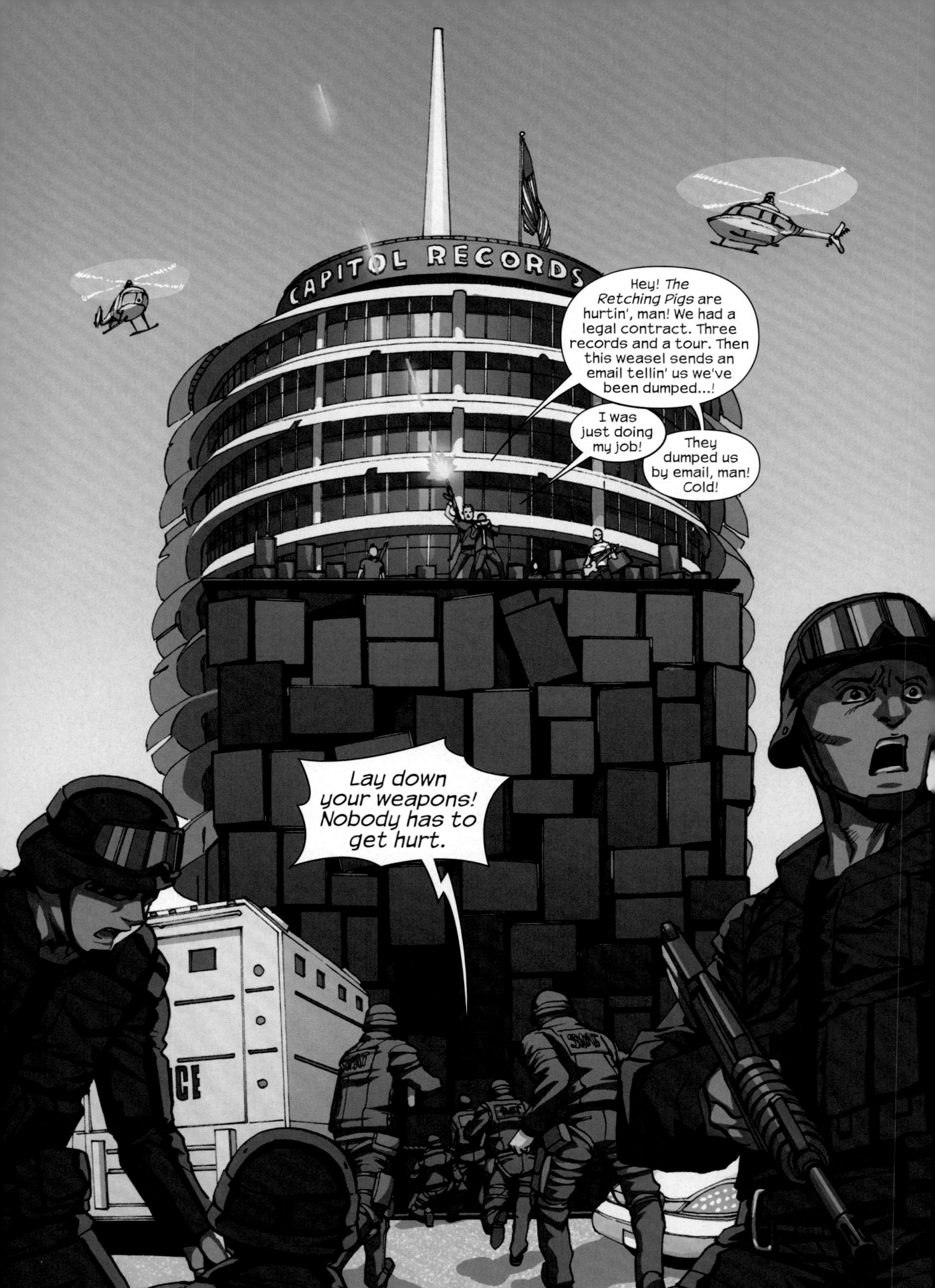
CAPITOL RECORDS
Hey! *The Retching Pigs* are hurtin', man! We had a legal contract. Three records and a tour. Then this weasel sends an email tellin' us we've been dumped...!
I was just doing my job!
They dumped us by email, man! Cold!
Lay down your weapons! Nobody has to get hurt.

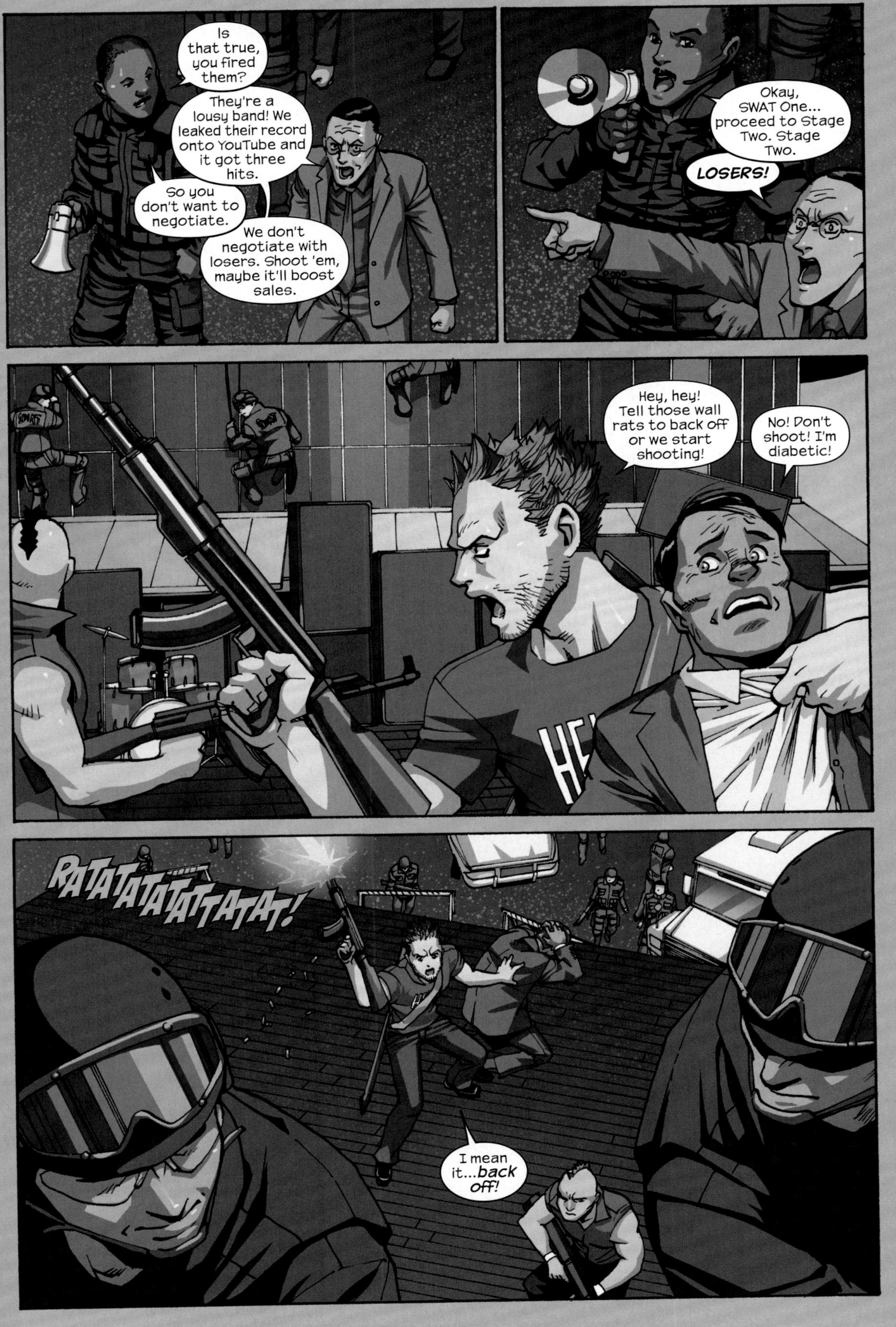

Is that true, you fired them?
They're a lousy band! We leaked their record onto YouTube and it got three hits.
So you don't want to negotiate.
We don't negotiate with losers. Shoot 'em, maybe it'll boost sales.
Okay, SWAT One... proceed to Stage Two. Stage Two.
LOSERS!
Hey, hey! Tell those wall rats to back off or we start shooting!
No! Don't shoot! I'm diabetic!
RATATATATATTATAT!
I mean it...*back off!*

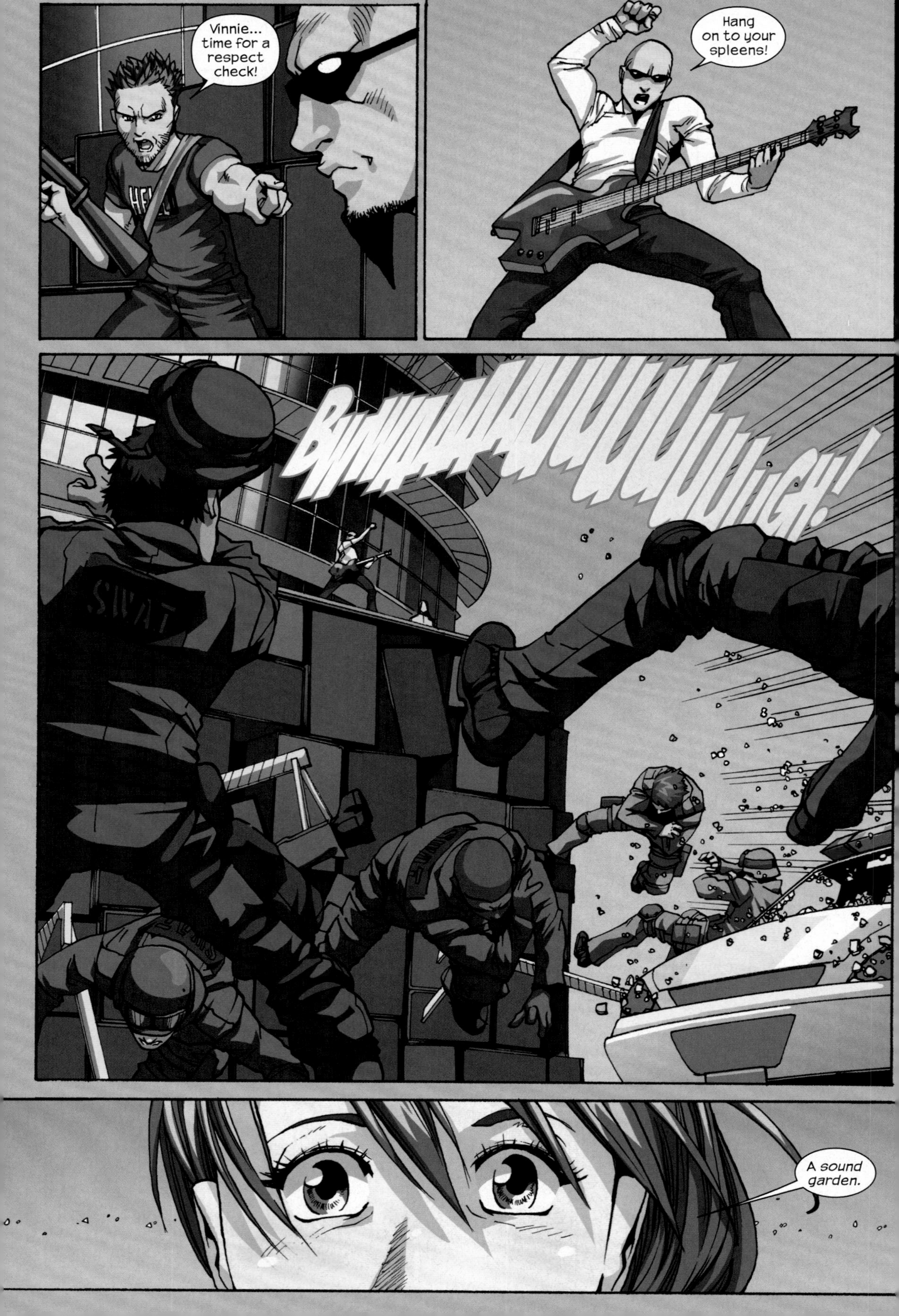
Vinnie... time for a respect check!
Hang on to your spleens!
BWWAAAAUUUUUUUUUGH!
A sound garden.

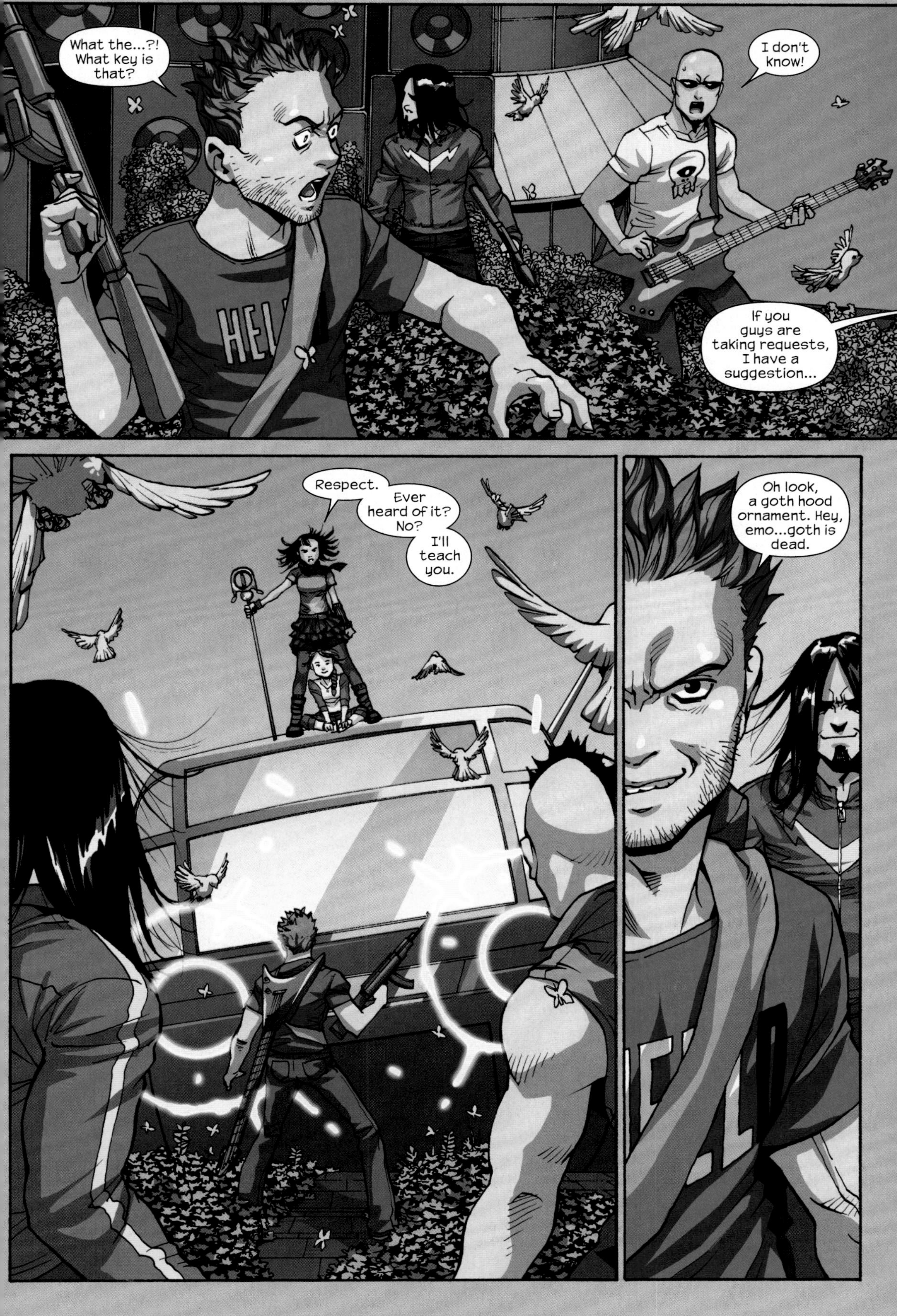
What the...?! What key is that?
I don't know!
If you guys are taking requests, I have a suggestion...
Respect.
Ever heard of it? No?
I'll teach you.
Oh look, a goth hood ornament. Hey, emo...goth is dead.

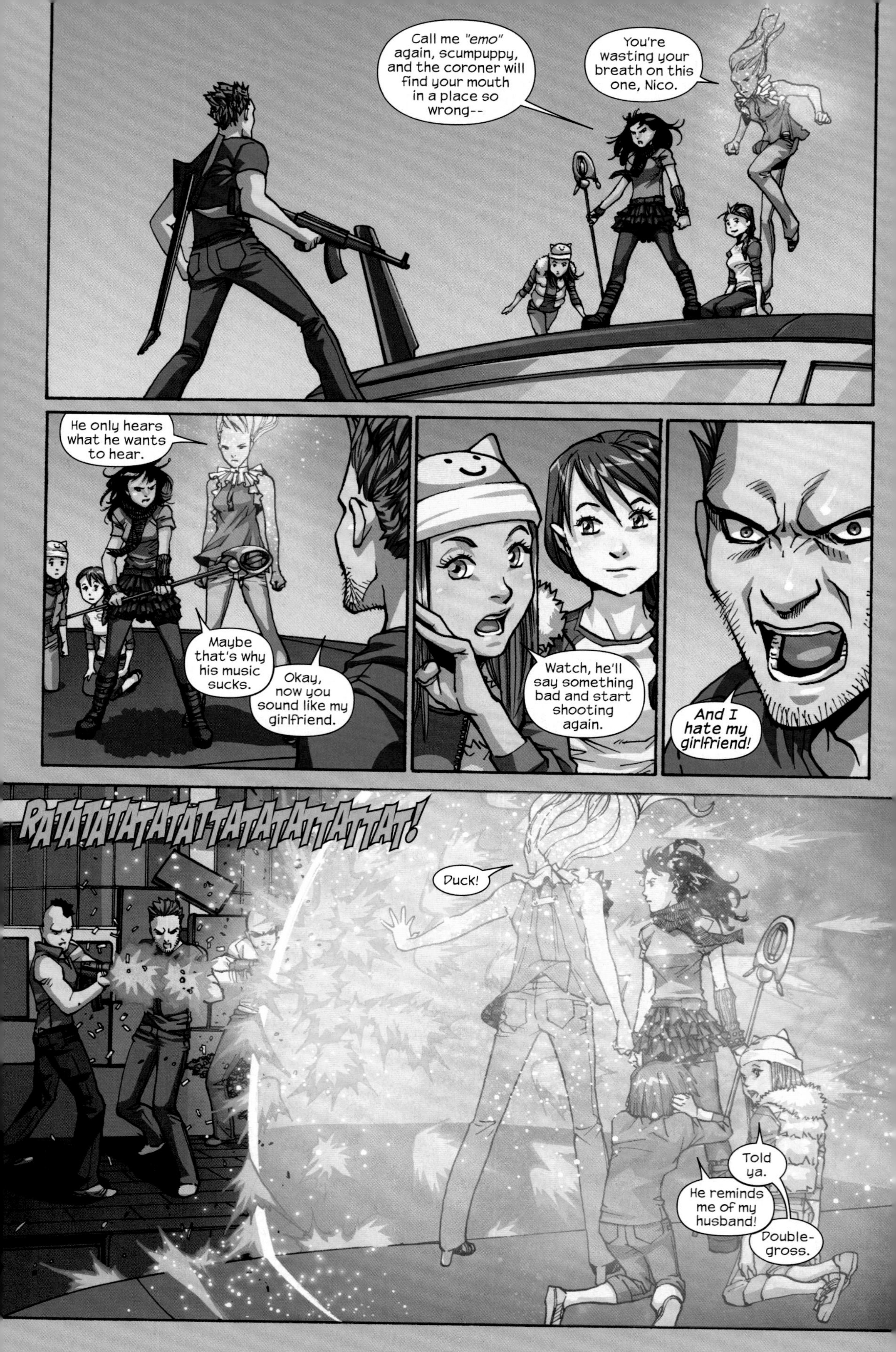
Call me *"emo"* again, scumpuppy, and the coroner will find your mouth in a place so wrong--
You're wasting your breath on this one, Nico.
He only hears what he wants to hear.
Maybe that's why his music sucks.
Okay, now you sound like my girlfriend.
Watch, he'll say something bad and start shooting again.
And I hate my girlfriend!
RATATATATATATTATATATTATTAT!
Duck!
Told ya.
He reminds me of my husband!
Double-gross.

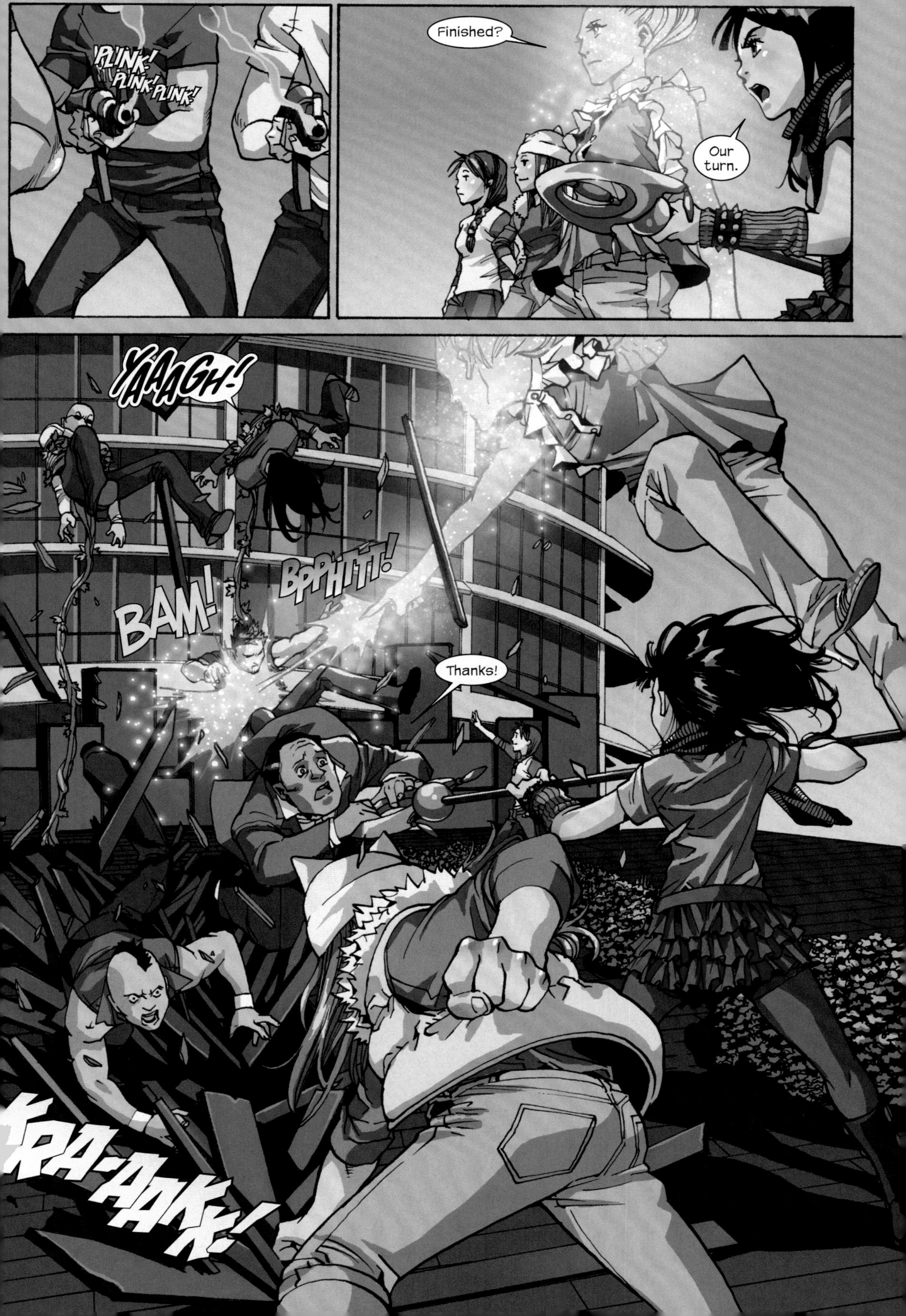
PLINK!
PLINK-PLINK-PLINK!
Finished?
Our turn.
YAAAGH!
BPPHTTT!
BAM!
Thanks!
KRA-AAKK!

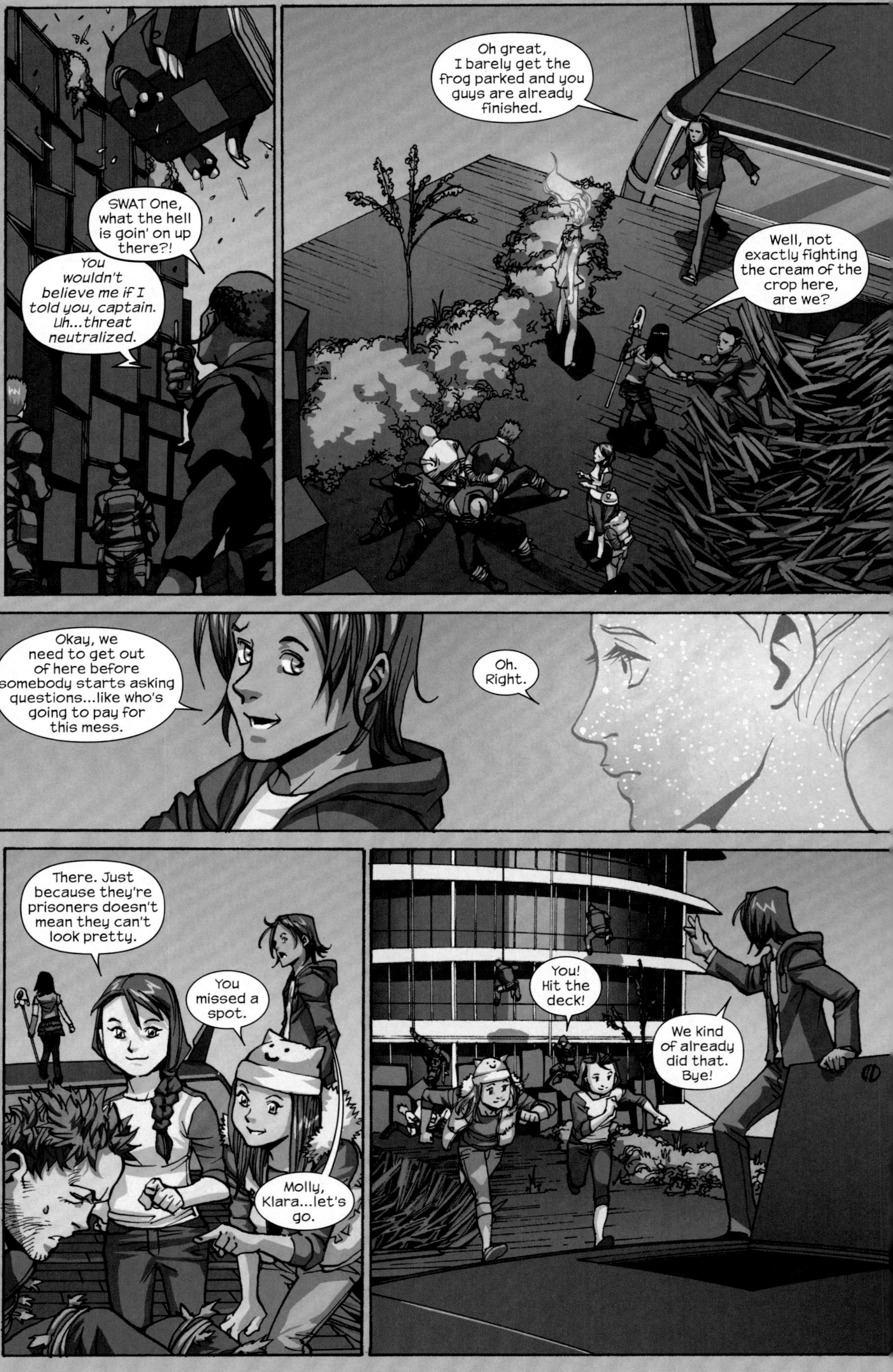
SWAT One, what the hell is goin' on up there?!
You wouldn't believe me if I told you, captain. Uh...threat neutralized.
Oh great, I barely get the frog parked and you guys are already finished.
Well, not exactly fighting the cream of the crop here, are we?
Okay, we need to get out of here before somebody starts asking questions...like who's going to pay for this mess.
Oh. Right.
There. Just because they're prisoners doesn't mean they can't look pretty.
You missed a spot.
Molly, Klara...let's go.
You! Hit the deck!
We kind of already did that. Bye!

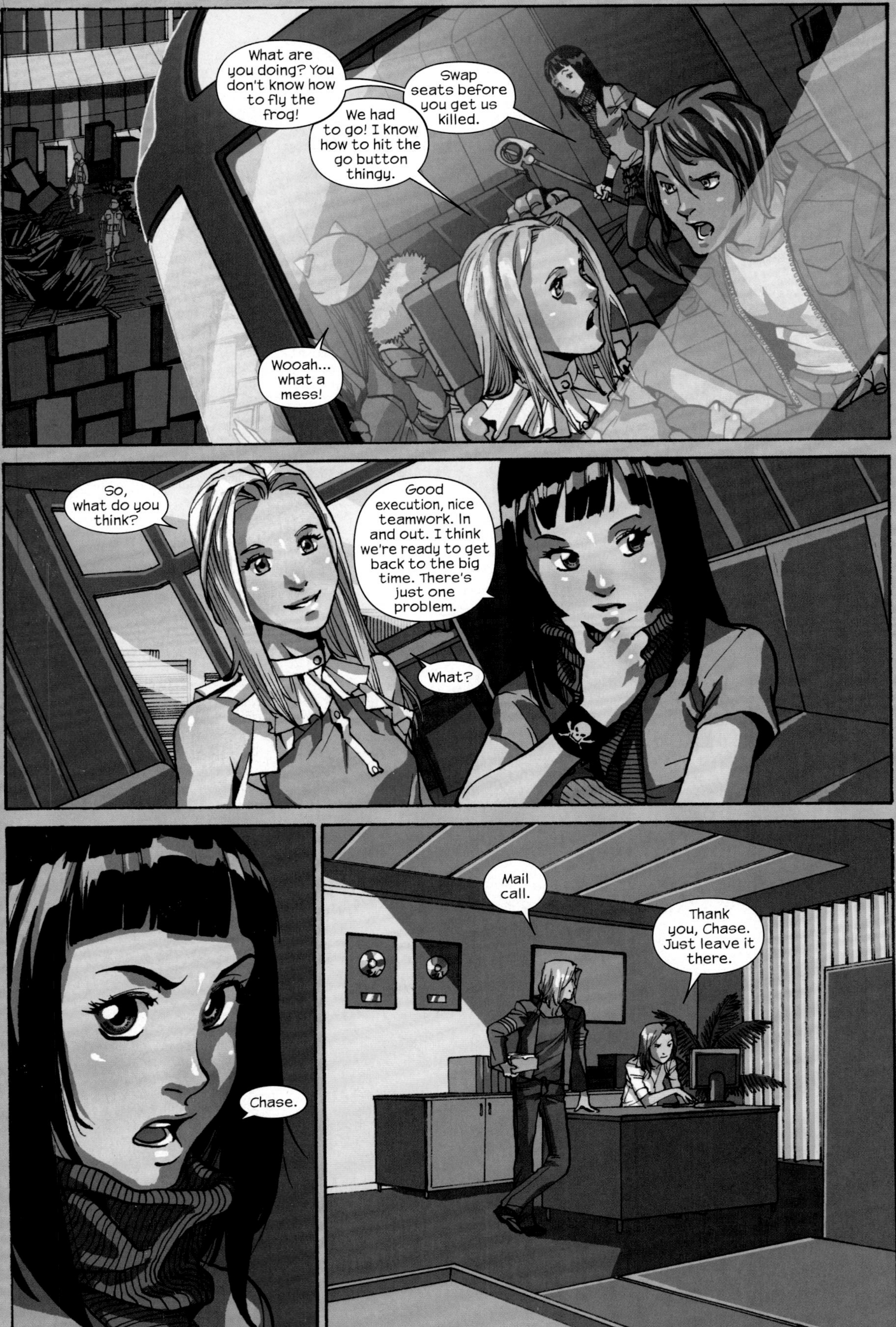
What are you doing? You don't know how to fly the frog!
Swap seats before you get us killed.
We had to go! I know how to hit the go button thingy.
Wooah... what a mess!
So, what do you think?
Good execution, nice teamwork. In and out. I think we're ready to get back to the big time. There's just one problem.
What?
Chase.
Mail call.
Thank you, Chase. Just leave it there.

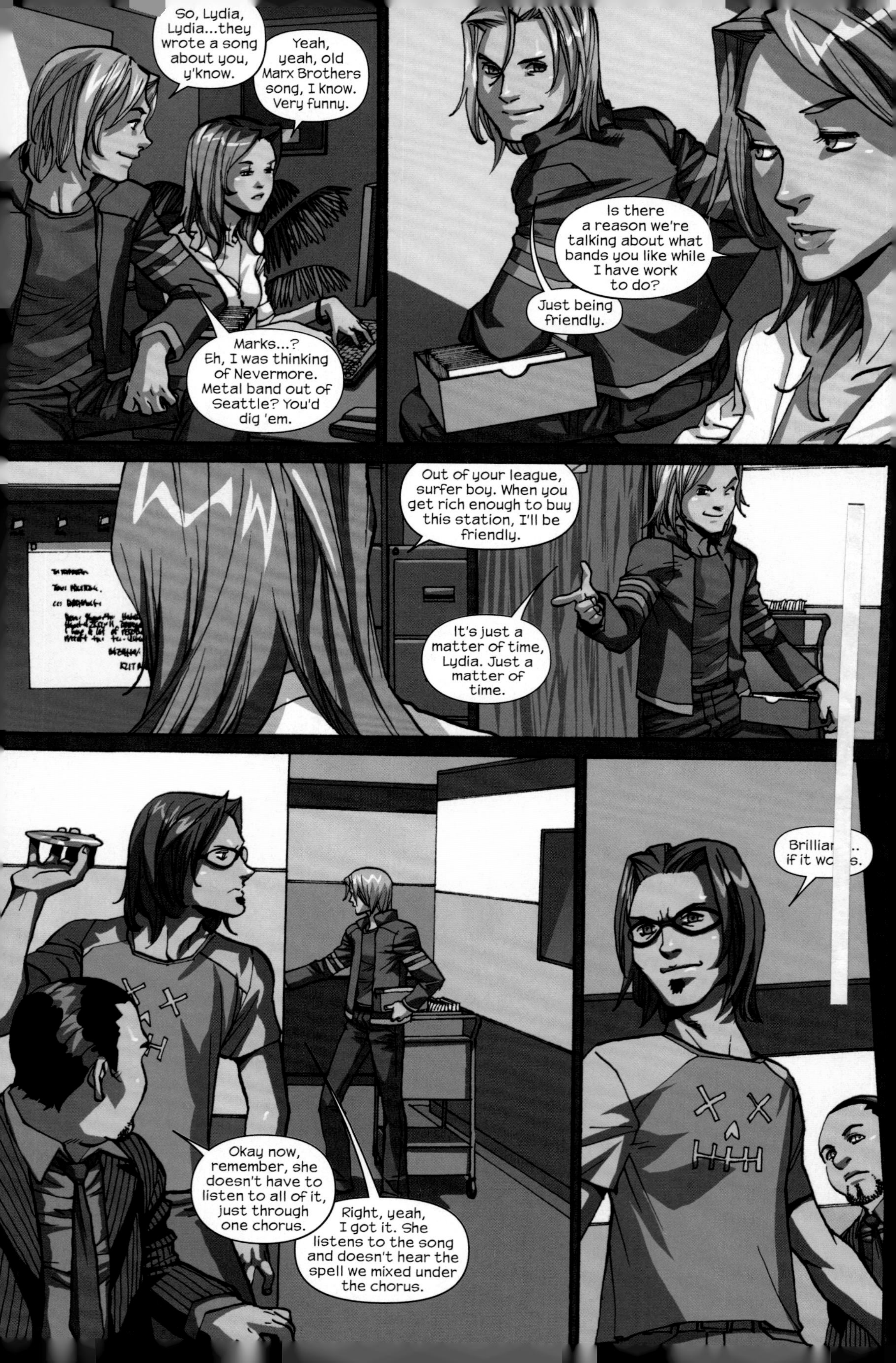

So, Lydia, Lydia...they wrote a song about you, y'know.
Yeah, yeah, old Marx Brothers song, I know. Very funny.
Marks...? Eh, I was thinking of Nevermore. Metal band out of Seattle? You'd dig 'em.
Is there a reason we're talking about what bands you like while I have work to do?
Just being friendly.
Out of your league, surfer boy. When you get rich enough to buy this station, I'll be friendly.
It's just a matter of time, Lydia. Just a matter of time.
Okay now, remember, she doesn't have to listen to all of it, just through one chorus.
Right, yeah, I got it. She listens to the song and doesn't hear the spell we mixed under the chorus.
Brillian
if it wo s.

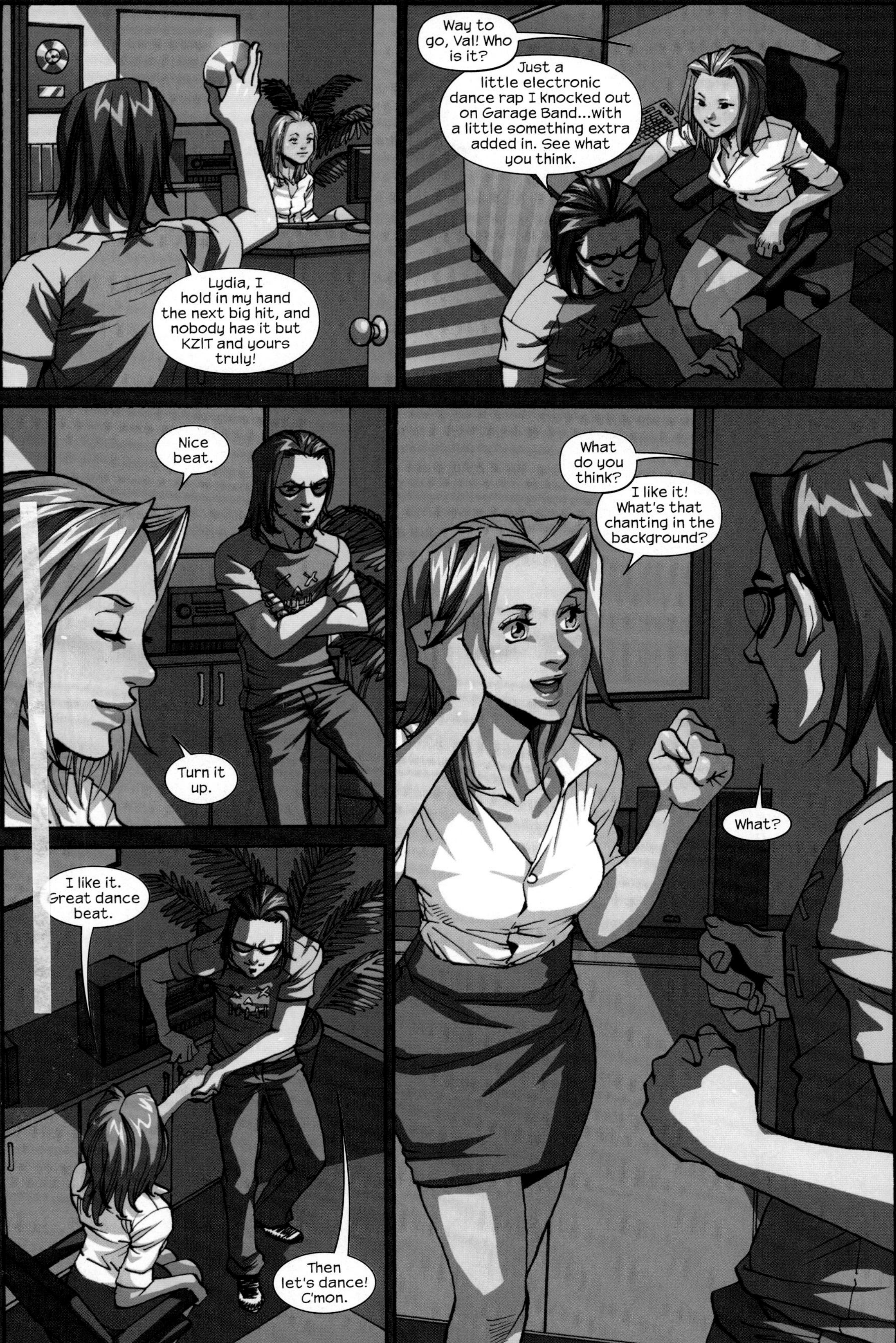

Lydia, I hold in my hand the next big hit, and nobody has it but KZIT and yours truly!
Way to go, Val! Who is it?
Just a little electronic dance rap I knocked out on Garage Band...with a little something extra added in. See what you think.
Nice beat.
Turn it up.
I like it. Great dance beat.
Then let's dance! C'mon.
What do you think?
I like it! What's that chanting in the background?
What?

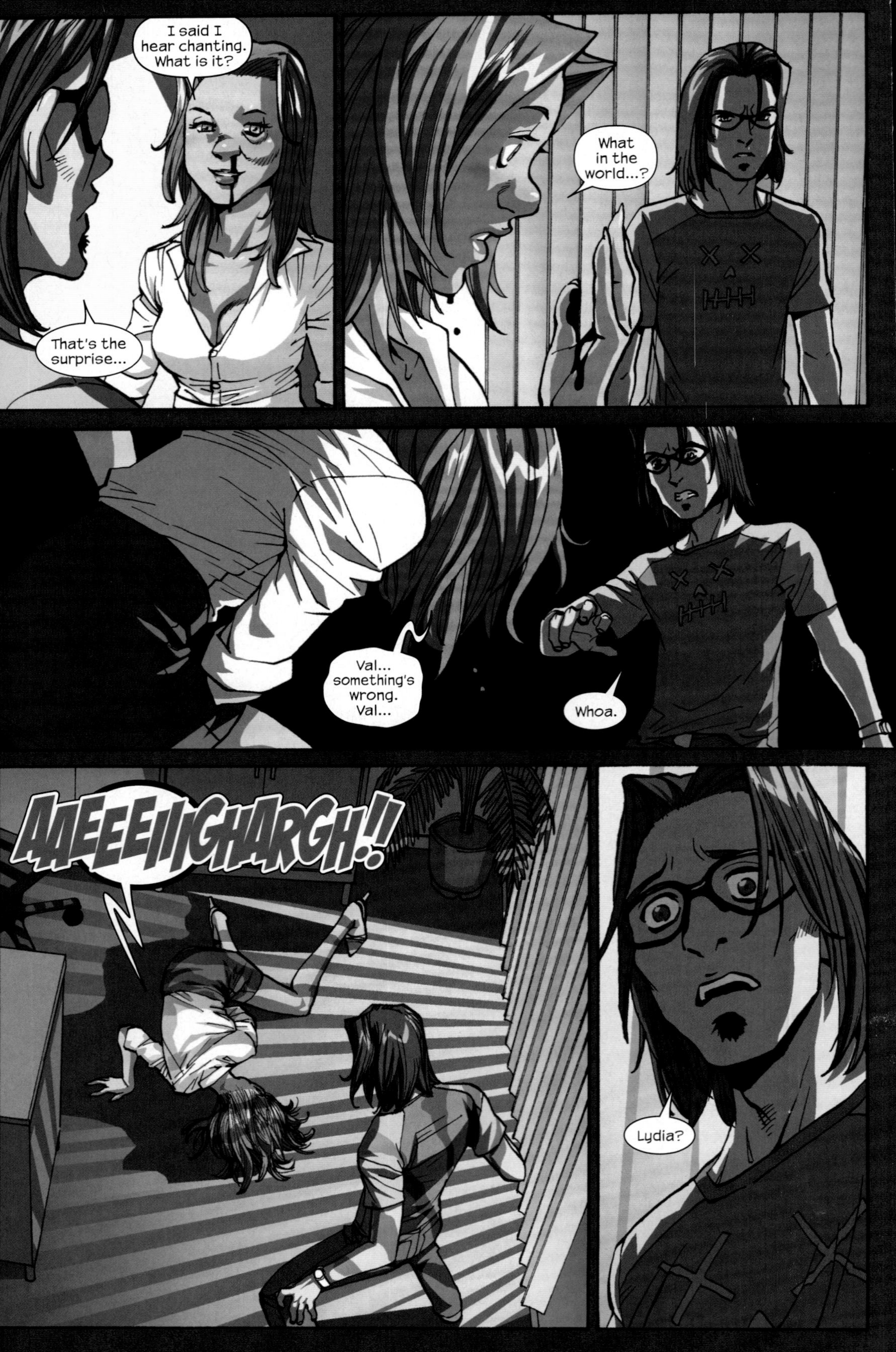
I said I hear chanting. What is it?
That's the surprise...
What in the world...?
Val... something's wrong. Val...
Whoa.
AAEEEIIIGHARGH!!
Lydia?

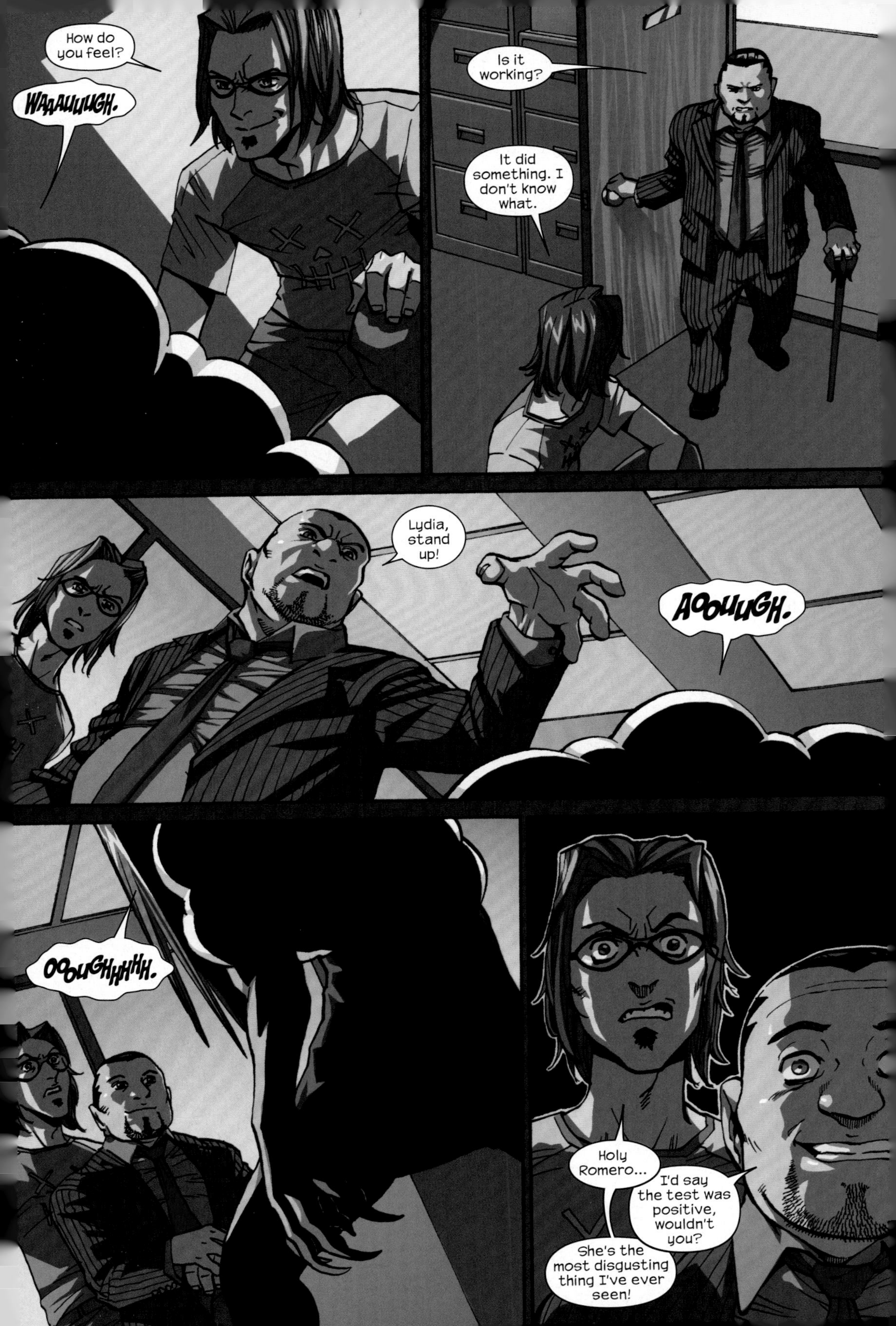
How do you feel?
WAAAUUUGH.
Is it working?
It did something. I don't know what.
Lydia, stand up!
AOOUUGH.
OOOUGHHHHH.
Holy Romero...
I'd say the test was positive, wouldn't you?
She's the most disgusting thing I've ever seen!

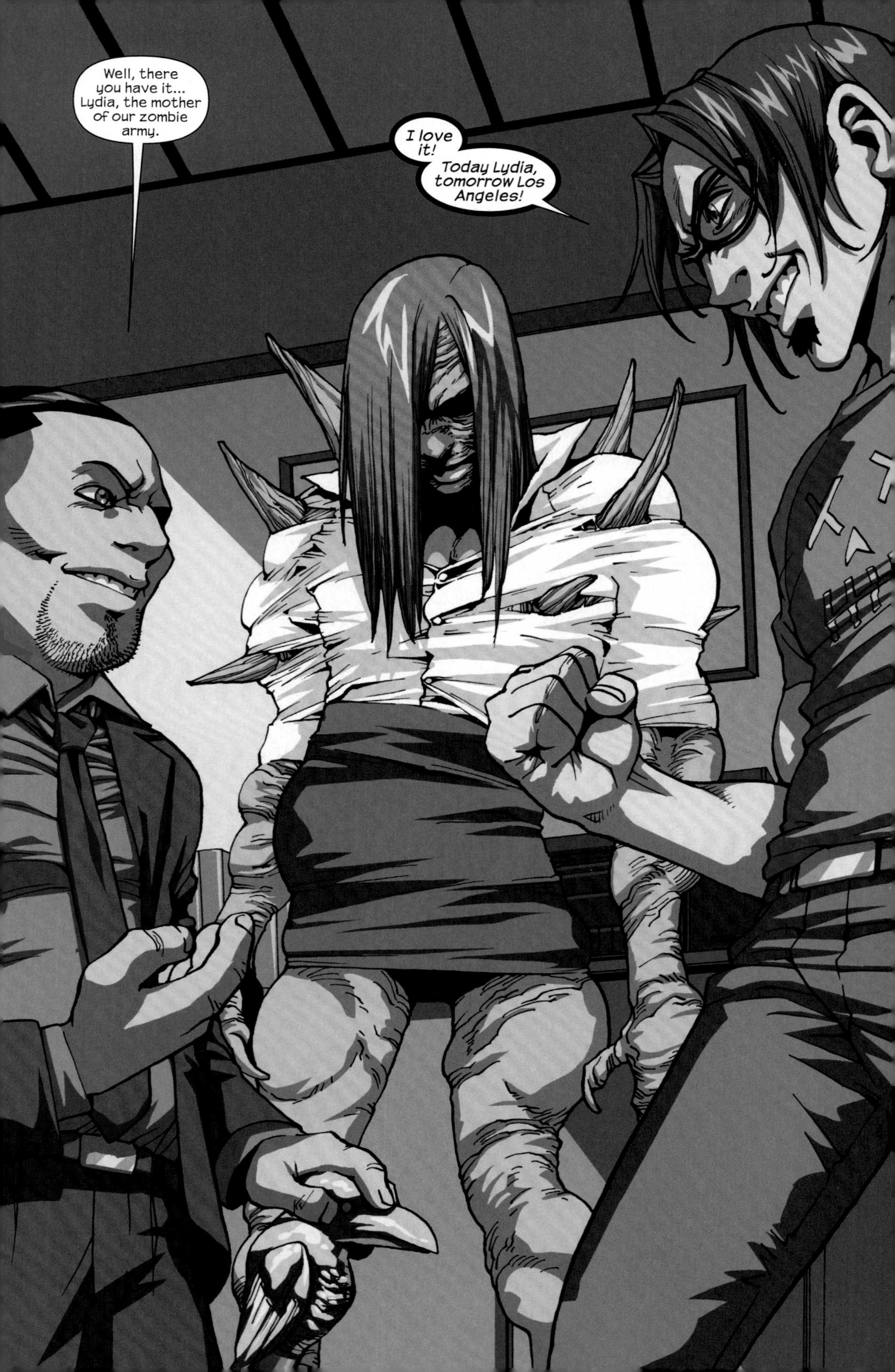
Well, there you have it... Lydia, the mother of our zombie army.
I love it!
Today Lydia, tomorrow Los Angeles!

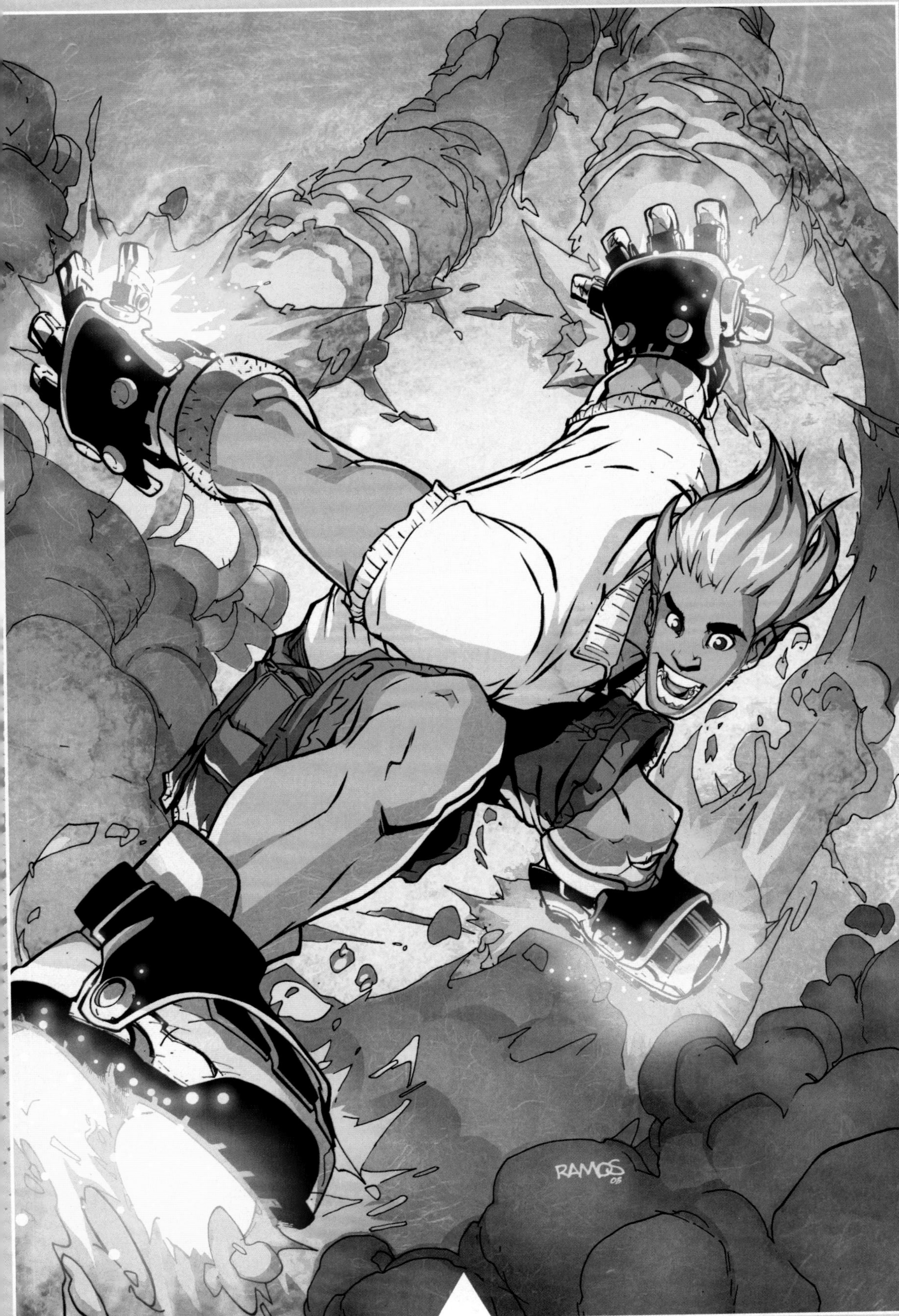
RAMOS
08

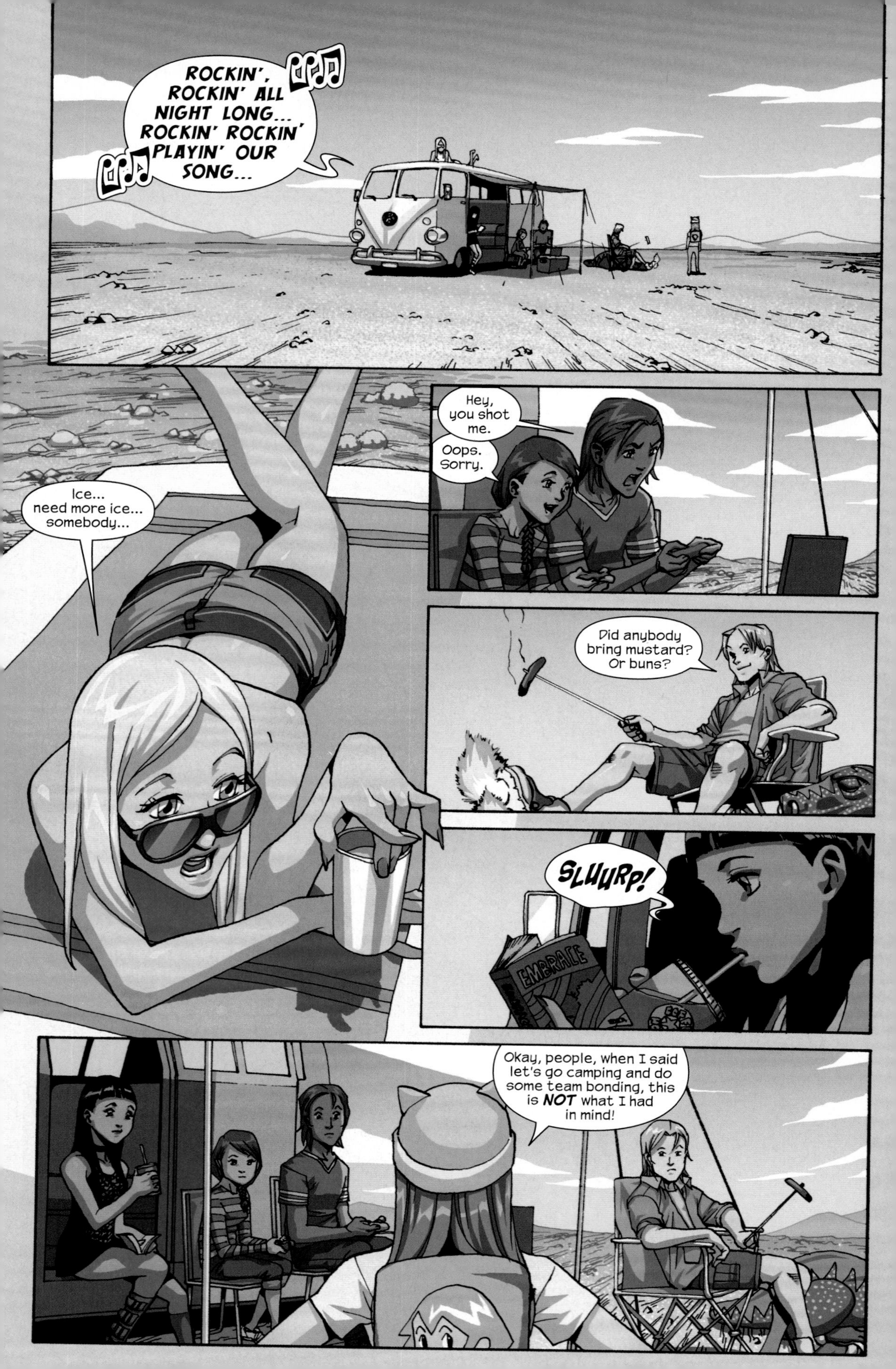
ROCKIN', ROCKIN' ALL NIGHT LONG... ROCKIN' ROCKIN' PLAYIN' OUR SONG...
Ice... need more ice... somebody...
Hey, you shot me.
Oops. Sorry.
Did anybody bring mustard? Or buns?
SLUURP!
EMBRACE
Okay, people, when I said let's go camping and do some team bonding, this is **NOT** what I had in mind!

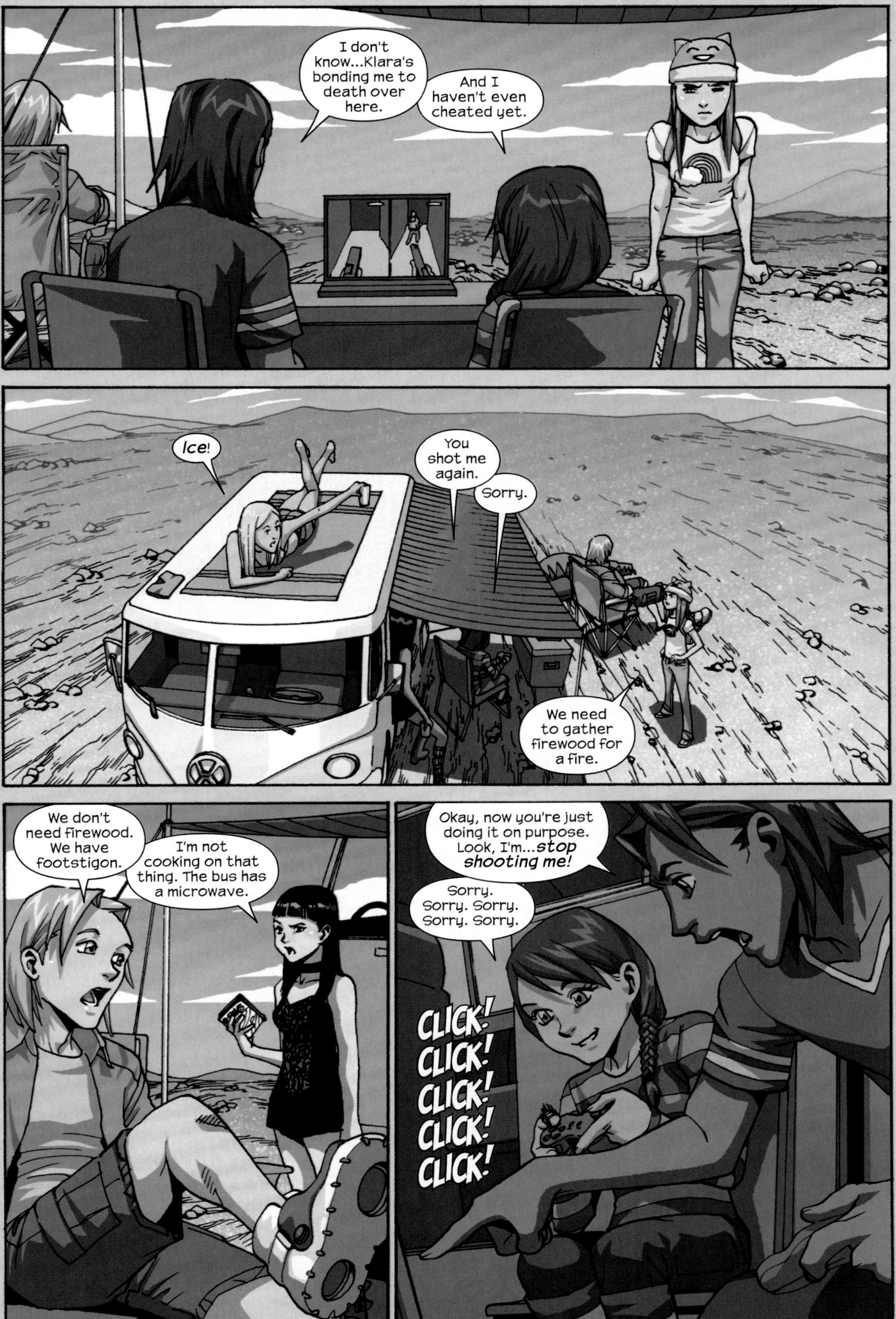
I don't know...Klara's bonding me to death over here.
And I haven't even cheated yet.
Ice!
You shot me again.
Sorry.
We need to gather firewood for a fire.
We don't need firewood. We have footstigon.
I'm not cooking on that thing. The bus has a microwave.
Okay, now you're just doing it on purpose. Look, I'm...*stop shooting me!*
Sorry. Sorry. Sorry. Sorry. Sorry.
CLICK! CLICK! CLICK! CLICK! CLICK!

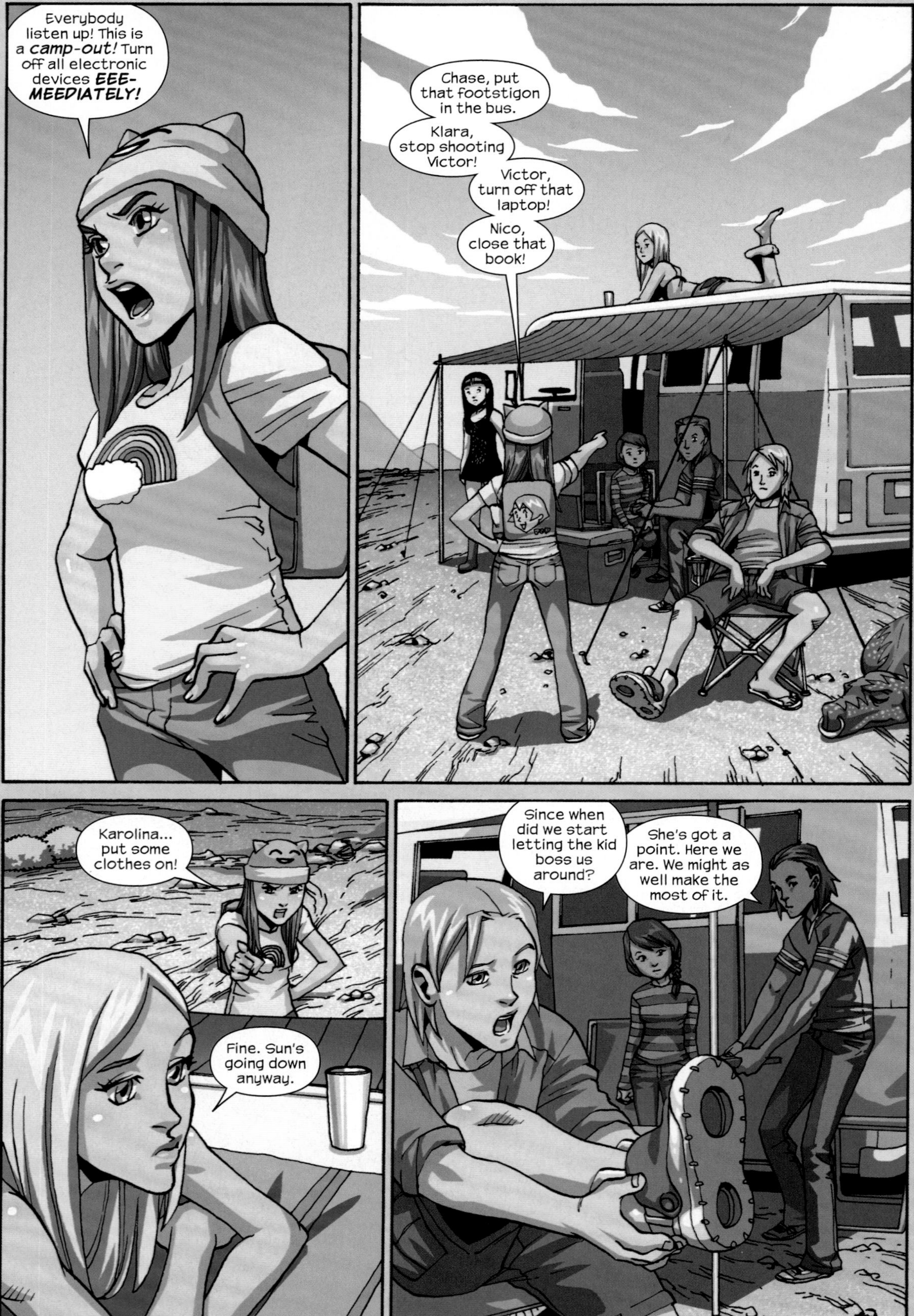

Everybody listen up! This is a *camp-out!* Turn off all electronic devices ***EEE-MEEDIATELY!***
Chase, put that footstigon in the bus.
Klara, stop shooting Victor!
Victor, turn off that laptop!
Nico, close that book!
Karolina... put some clothes on!
Fine. Sun's going down anyway.
Since when did we start letting the kid boss us around?
She's got a point. Here we are. We might as well make the most of it.

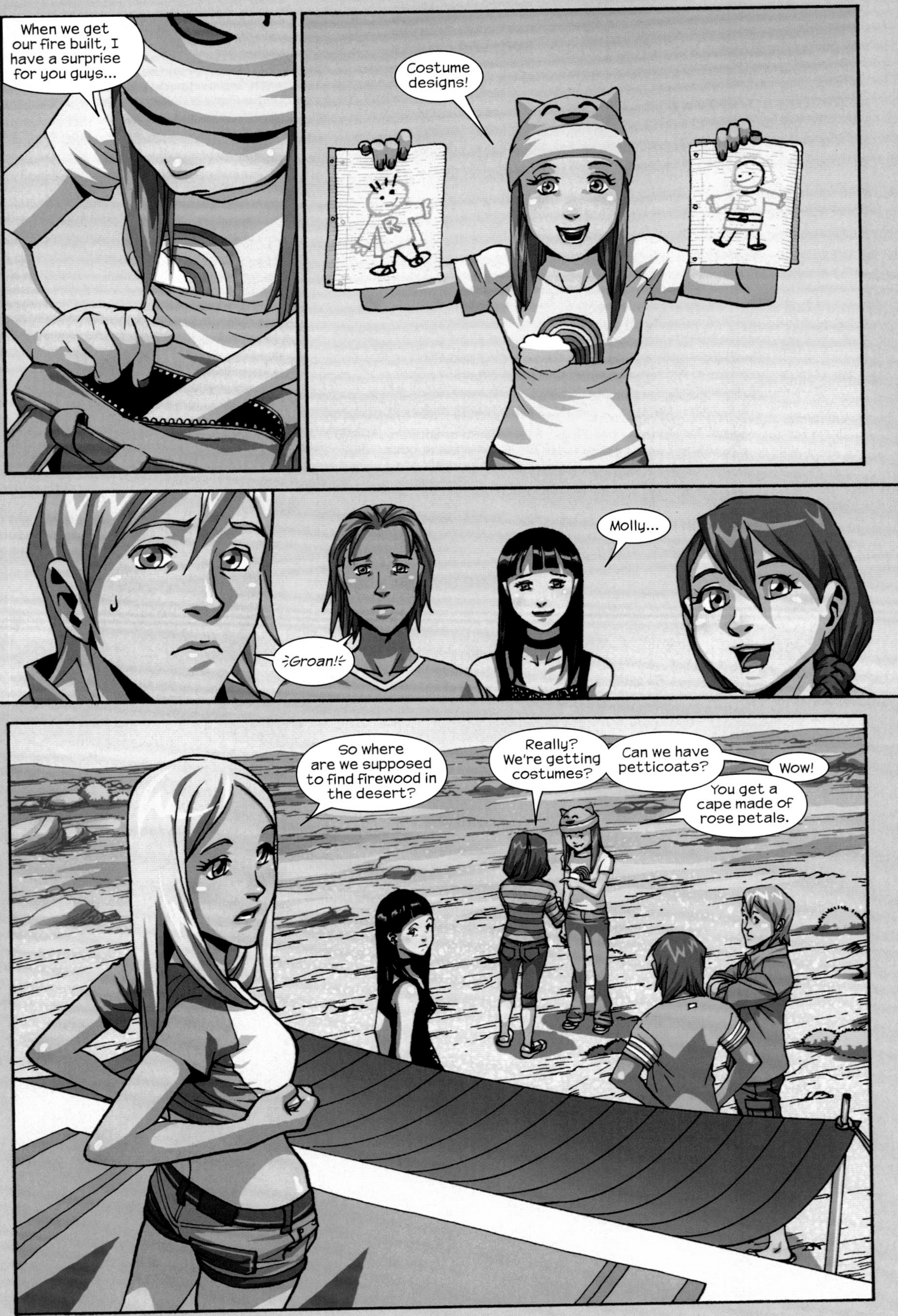
When we get our fire built, I have a surprise for you guys...
Costume designs!
R
Molly...
Groan!
So where are we supposed to find firewood in the desert?
Really? We're getting costumes?
Can we have petticoats?
Wow!
You get a cape made of rose petals.

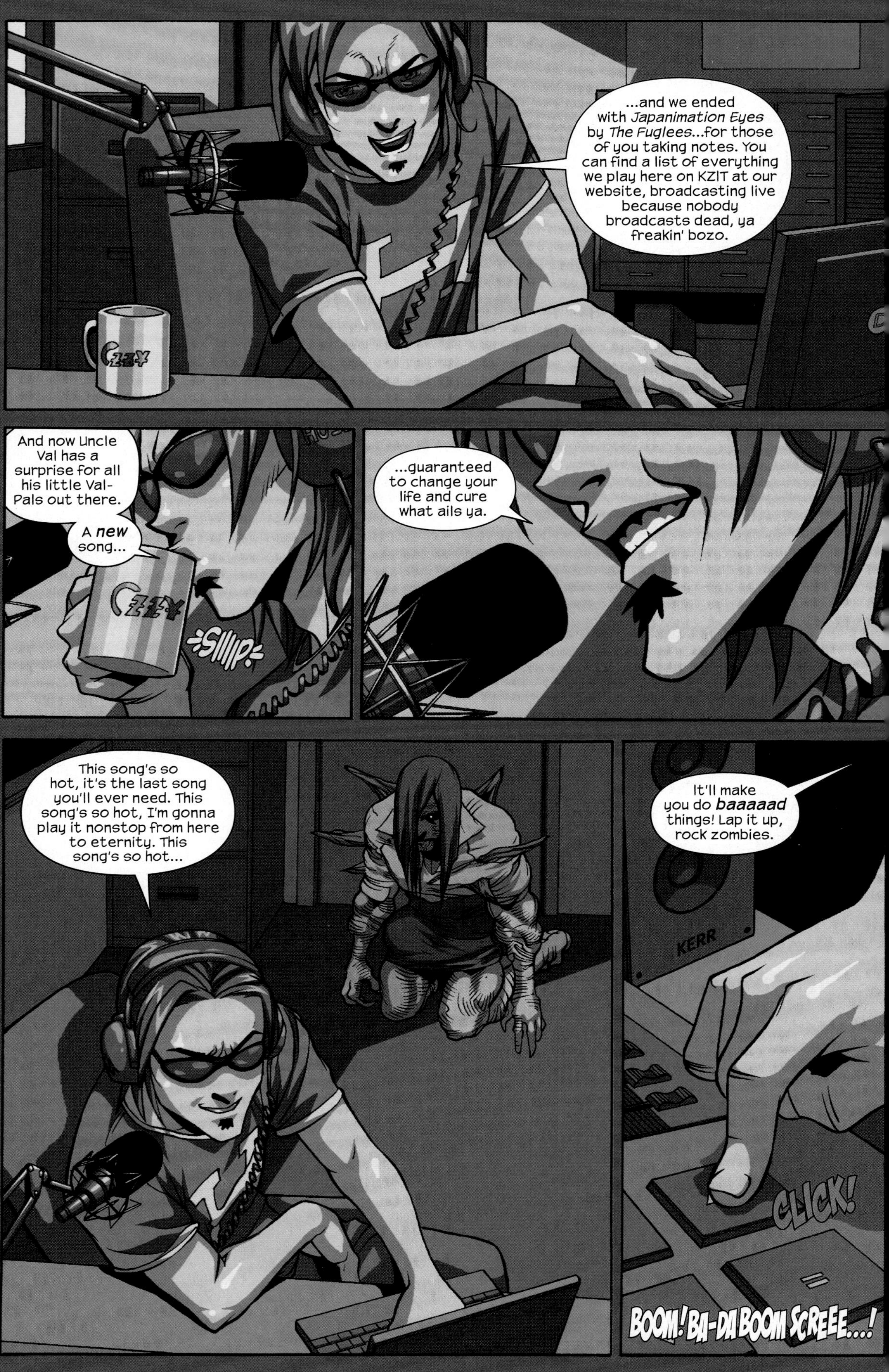
...and we ended with *Japanimation Eyes* by *The Fuglees*...for those of you taking notes. You can find a list of everything we play here on KZIT at our website, broadcasting live because nobody broadcasts dead, ya freakin' bozo.
And now Uncle Val has a surprise for all his little Val-Pals out there.
A ***new*** song...
SLLLP
...guaranteed to change your life and cure what ails ya.
This song's so hot, it's the last song you'll ever need. This song's so hot, I'm gonna play it nonstop from here to eternity. This song's so hot...
It'll make you do ***baaaaad*** things! Lap it up, rock zombies.
KERR
CLICK!
BOOM! BA-DA BOOM SCREEE...!

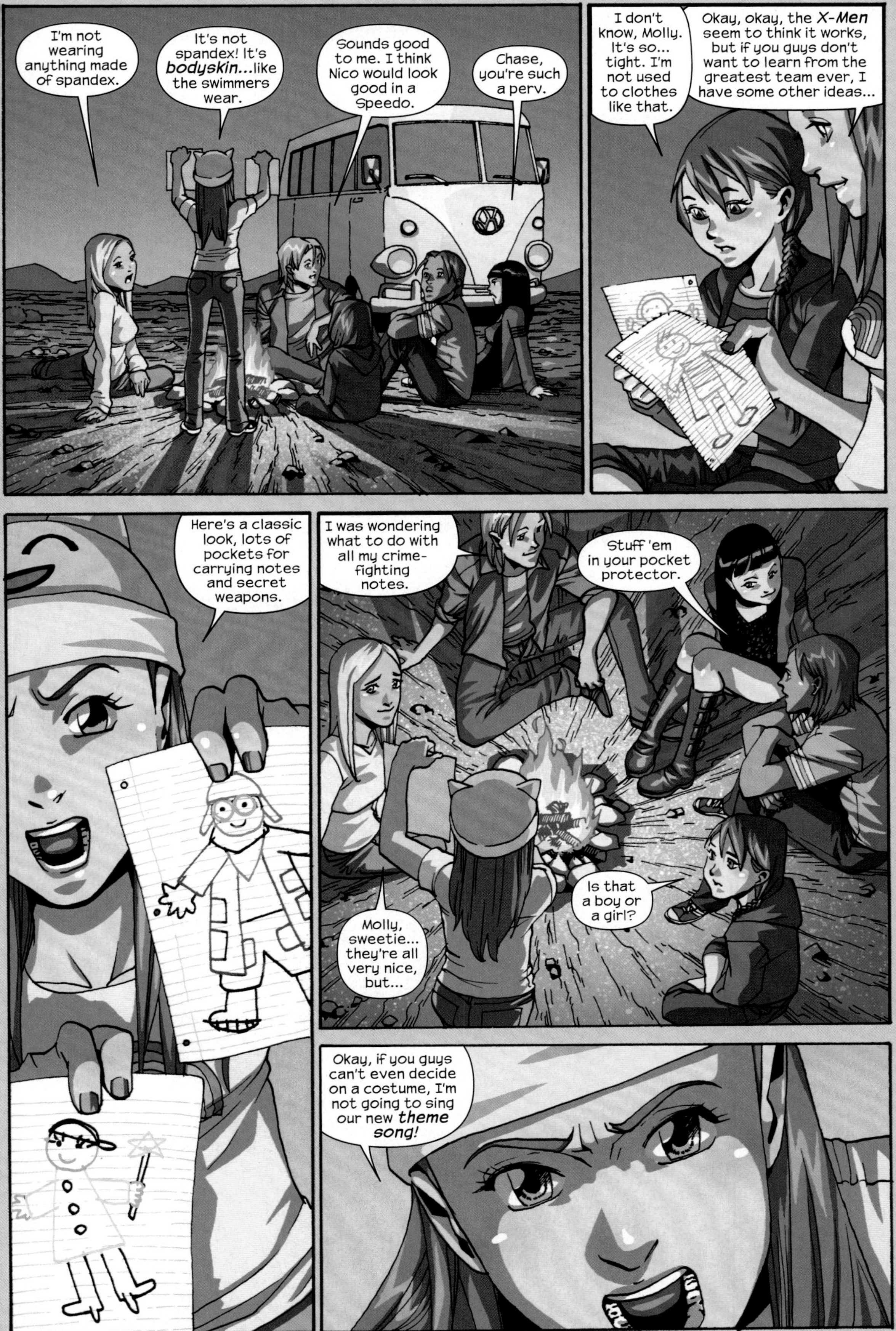
I'm not wearing anything made of spandex.
It's not spandex! It's *bodyskin...*like the swimmers wear.
Sounds good to me. I think Nico would look good in a Speedo.
Chase, you're such a perv.
I don't know, Molly. It's so... tight. I'm not used to clothes like that.
Okay, okay, the *X-Men* seem to think it works, but if you guys don't want to learn from the greatest team ever, I have some other ideas...
Here's a classic look, lots of pockets for carrying notes and secret weapons.
I was wondering what to do with all my crime-fighting notes.
Stuff 'em in your pocket protector.
Is that a boy or a girl?
Molly, sweetie... they're all very nice, but...
Okay, if you guys can't even decide on a costume, I'm not going to sing our new *theme song!*

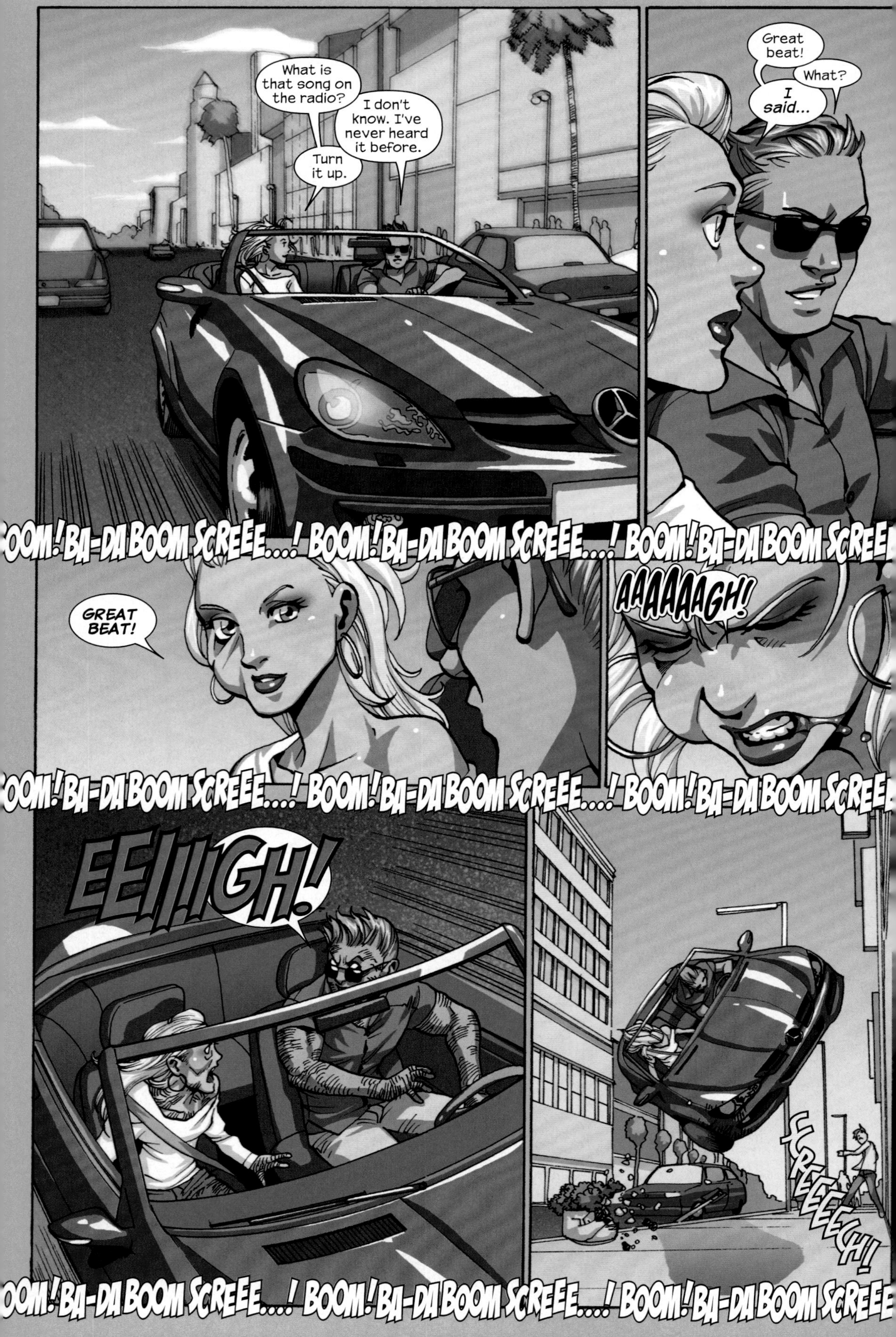
What is that song on the radio?
Turn it up.
I don't know. I've never heard it before.
Great beat!
What?
I said...
BOOM! BA-DA BOOM SCREEE...! BOOM! BA-DA BOOM SCREEE...! BOOM! BA-DA BOOM SCREE
GREAT BEAT!
AAAAAAGH!
BOOM! BA-DA BOOM SCREEE...! BOOM! BA-DA BOOM SCREEE...! BOOM! BA-DA BOOM SCREE
EEIIIIGH!
SCREEEECH!
BOOM! BA-DA BOOM SCREEE...! BOOM! BA-DA BOOM SCREEE...! BOOM! BA-DA BOOM SCREEE

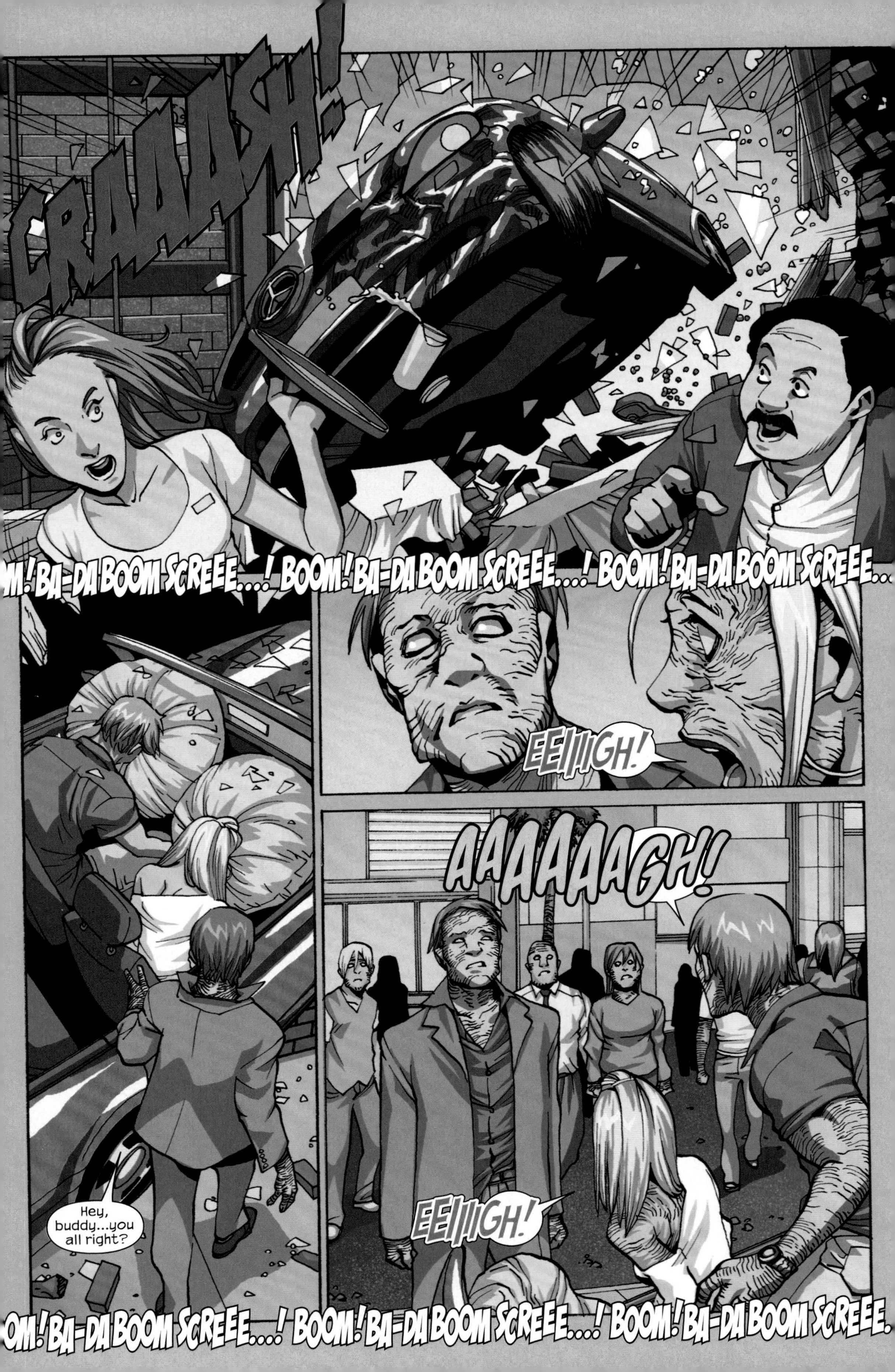
CRAAASH!
M! BA-DA BOOM SCREEE...! BOOM! BA-DA BOOM SCREEE...! BOOM! BA-DA BOOM SCREEE...
EEIIIIGH!
Hey, buddy...you all right?
AAAAAAAGH!
EEIIIIGH!
OM! BA-DA BOOM SCREEE...! BOOM! BA-DA BOOM SCREEE...! BOOM! BA-DA BOOM SCREEE.

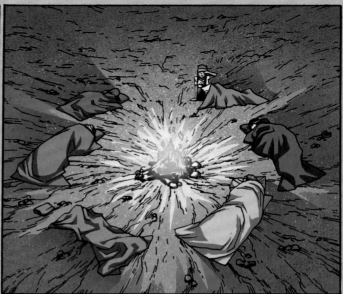

Mornin'.

Hey, K.

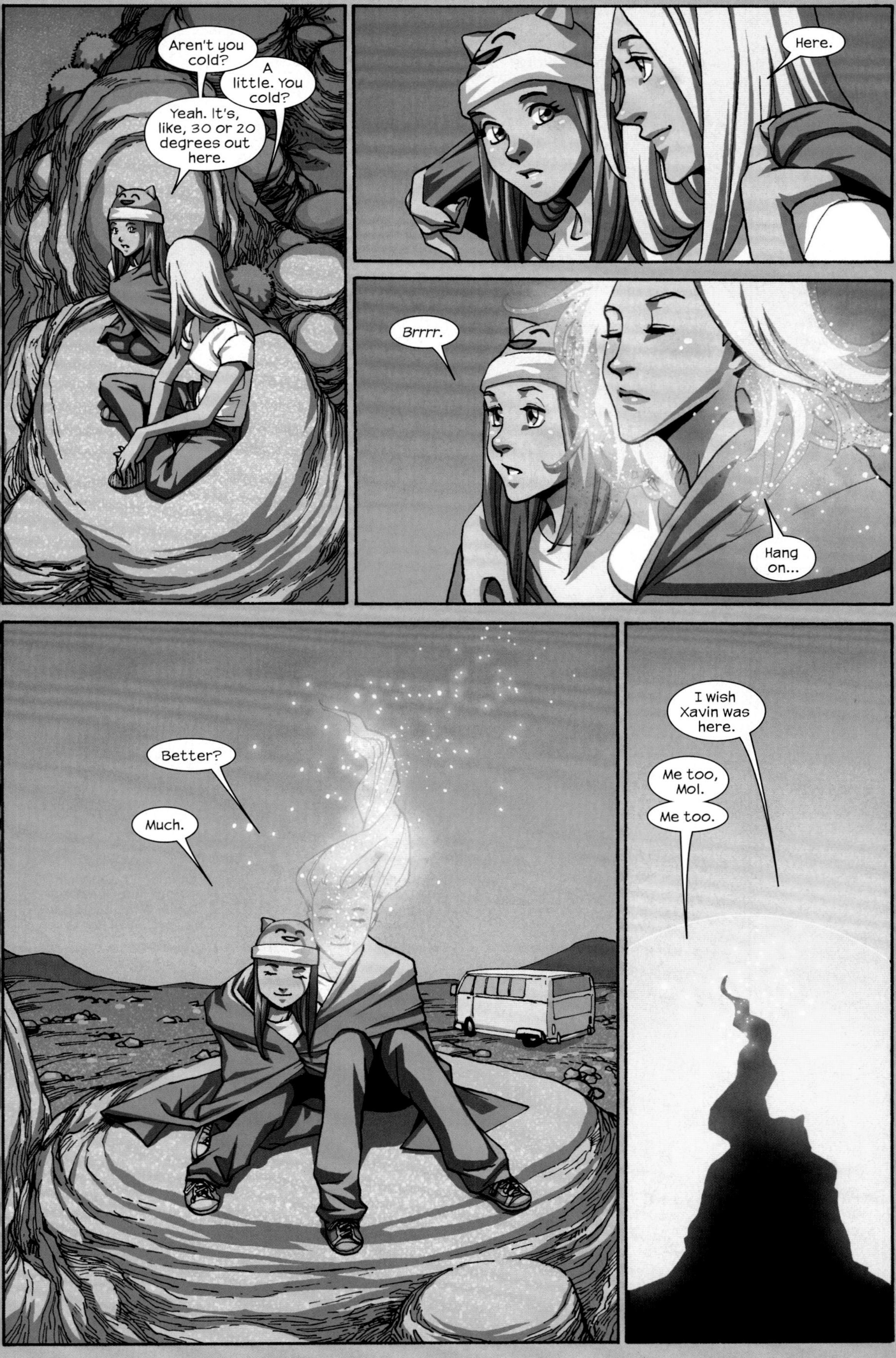
Aren't you cold?
A little. You cold?
Yeah. It's, like, 30 or 20 degrees out here.
Here.
Brrrr.
Hang on...
Better?
Much.
I wish Xavin was here.
Me too, Mol.
Me too.

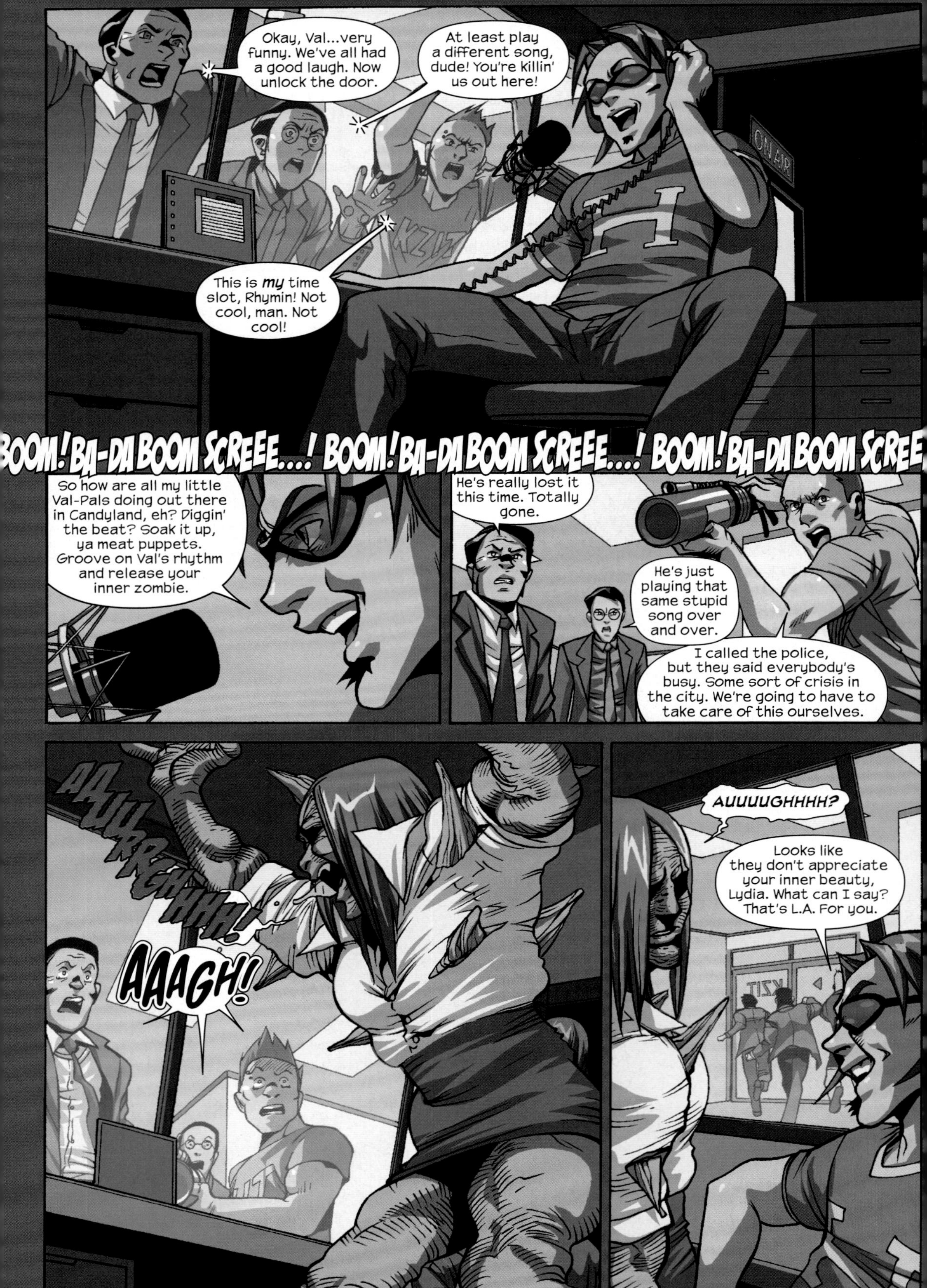
Okay, Val...very funny. We've all had a good laugh. Now unlock the door.
At least play a different song, dude! You're killin' us out here!
ON AIR
KZIT
This is my time slot, Rhymin! Not cool, man. Not cool!
BOOM! BA-DA BOOM SCREEE...! BOOM! BA-DA BOOM SCREEE...! BOOM! BA-DA BOOM SCREE
So how are all my little Val-Pals doing out there in Candyland, eh? Diggin' the beat? Soak it up, ya meat puppets. Groove on Val's rhythm and release your inner zombie.
He's really lost it this time. Totally gone.
He's just playing that same stupid song over and over.
I called the police, but they said everybody's busy. Some sort of crisis in the city. We're going to have to take care of this ourselves.
AAUURGHHHH!
AAAGH!
AUUUUGHHHH?
Looks like they don't appreciate your inner beauty, Lydia. What can I say? That's L.A. For you.
KZIT

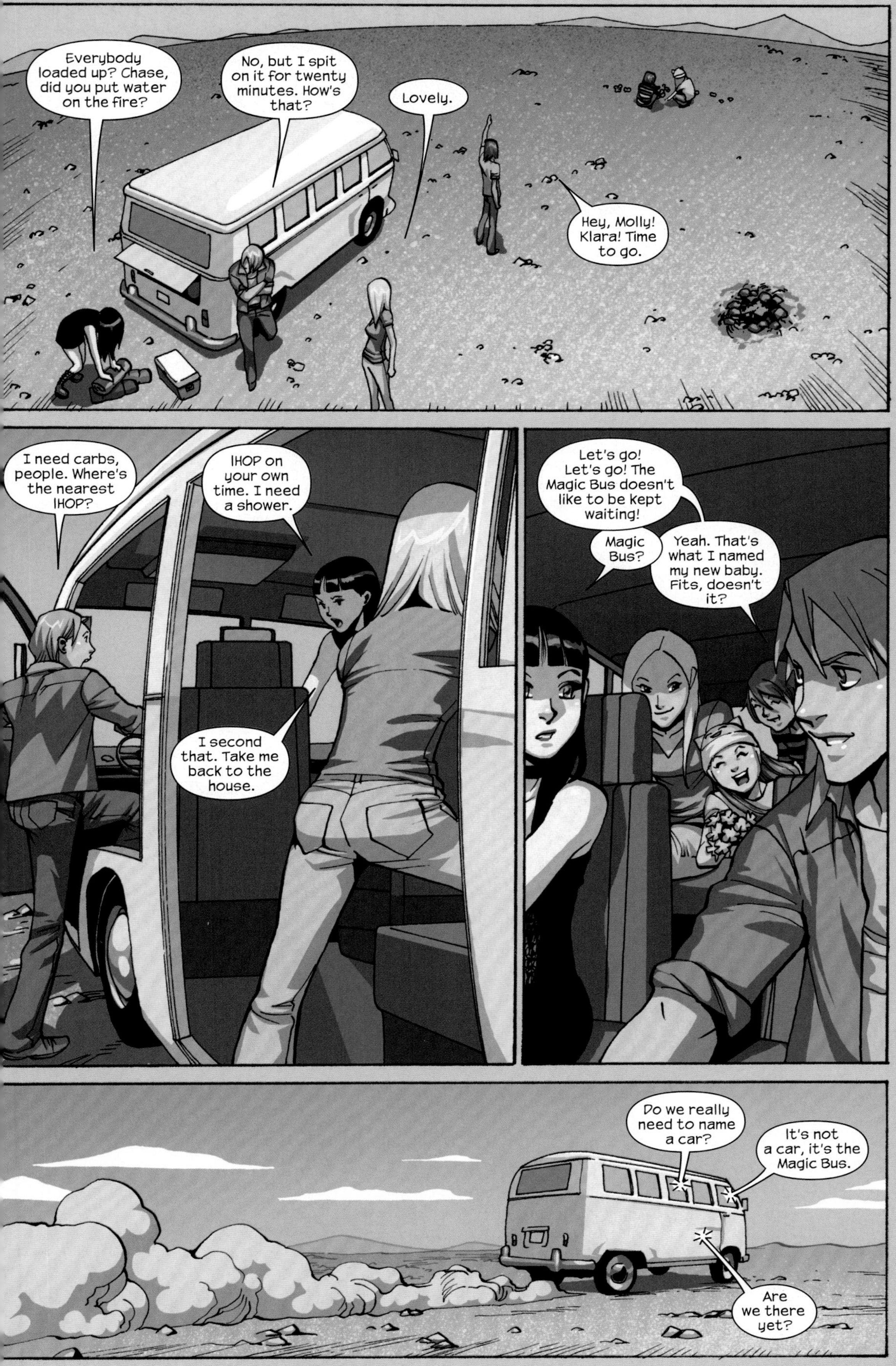

Everybody loaded up? Chase, did you put water on the fire?
No, but I spit on it for twenty minutes. How's that?
Lovely.
Hey, Molly! Klara! Time to go.
I need carbs, people. Where's the nearest IHOP?
IHOP on your own time. I need a shower.
I second that. Take me back to the house.
Let's go! Let's go! The Magic Bus doesn't like to be kept waiting!
Magic Bus?
Yeah. That's what I named my new baby. Fits, doesn't it?
Do we really need to name a car?
It's not a car, it's the Magic Bus.
Are we there yet?

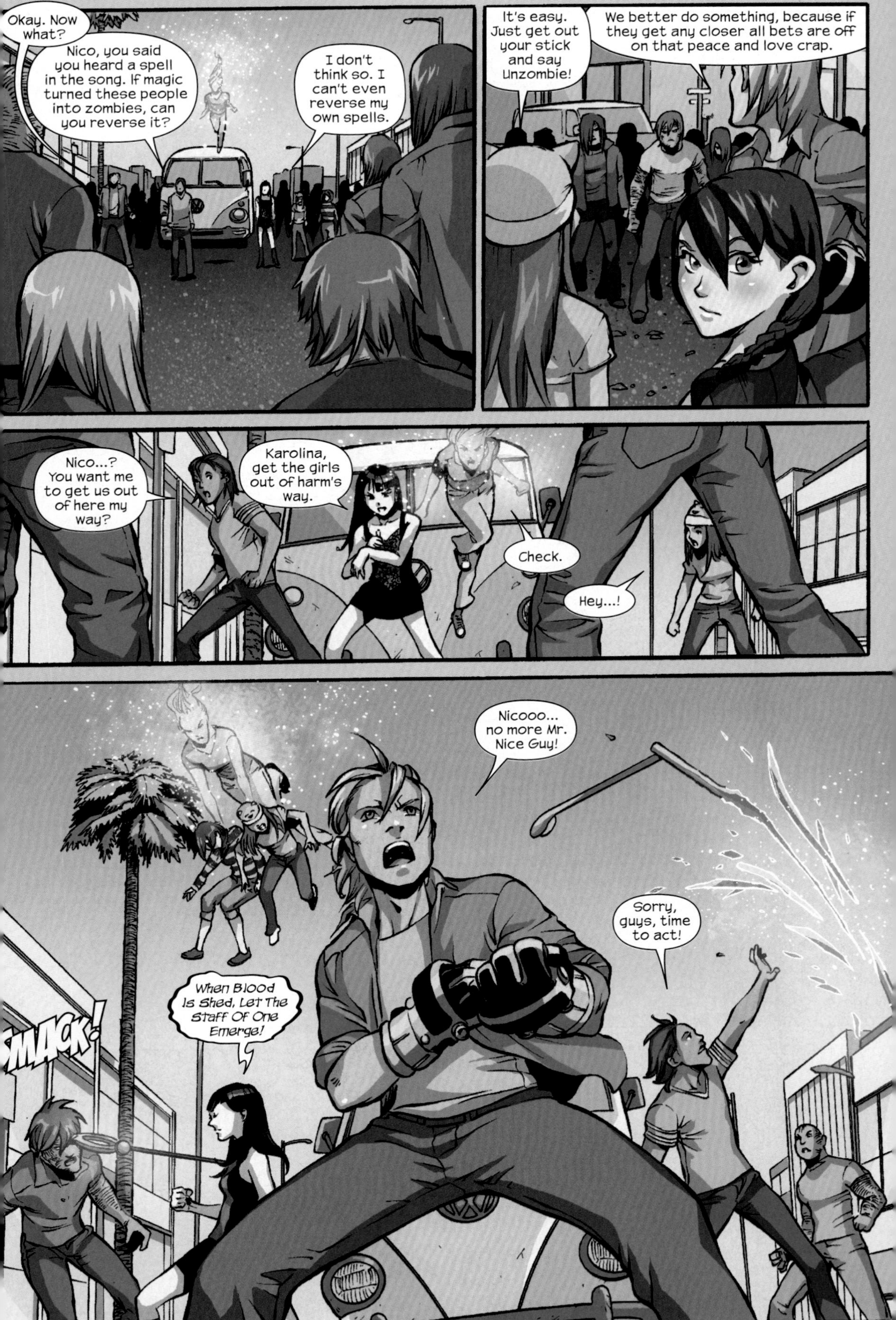
Okay. Now what?
Nico, you said you heard a spell in the song. If magic turned these people into zombies, can you reverse it?
I don't think so. I can't even reverse my own spells.
It's easy. Just get out your stick and say Unzombie!
We better do something, because if they get any closer all bets are off on that peace and love crap.
Nico...? You want me to get us out of here my way?
Karolina, get the girls out of harm's way.
Check.
Hey...!
Nicooo... no more Mr. Nice Guy!
Sorry, guys, time to act!
When Blood Is Shed, Let The Staff Of One Emerge!
SMACK!

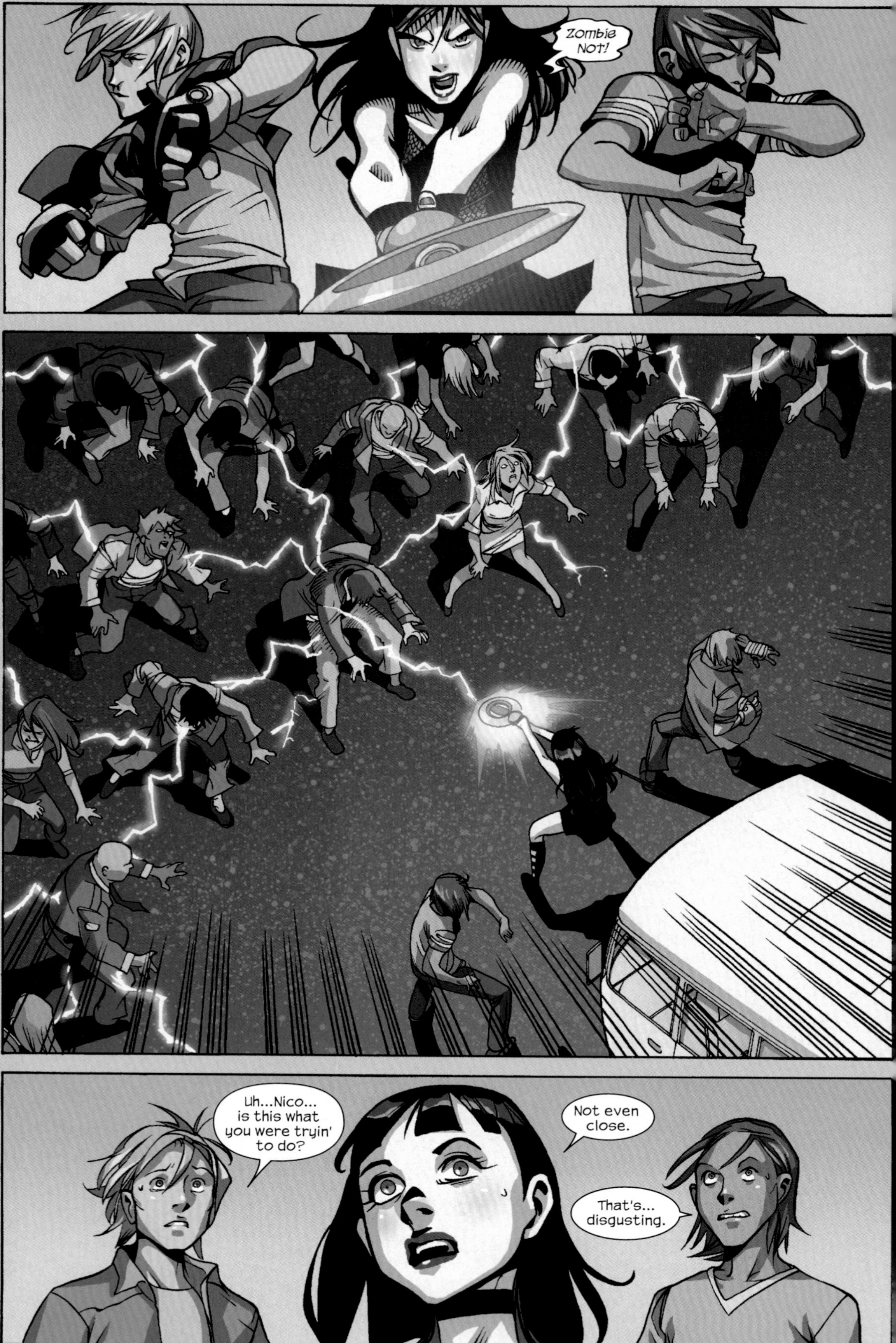
Zombie Not!
Uh...Nico... is this what you were tryin' to do?
Not even close.
That's... disgusting.

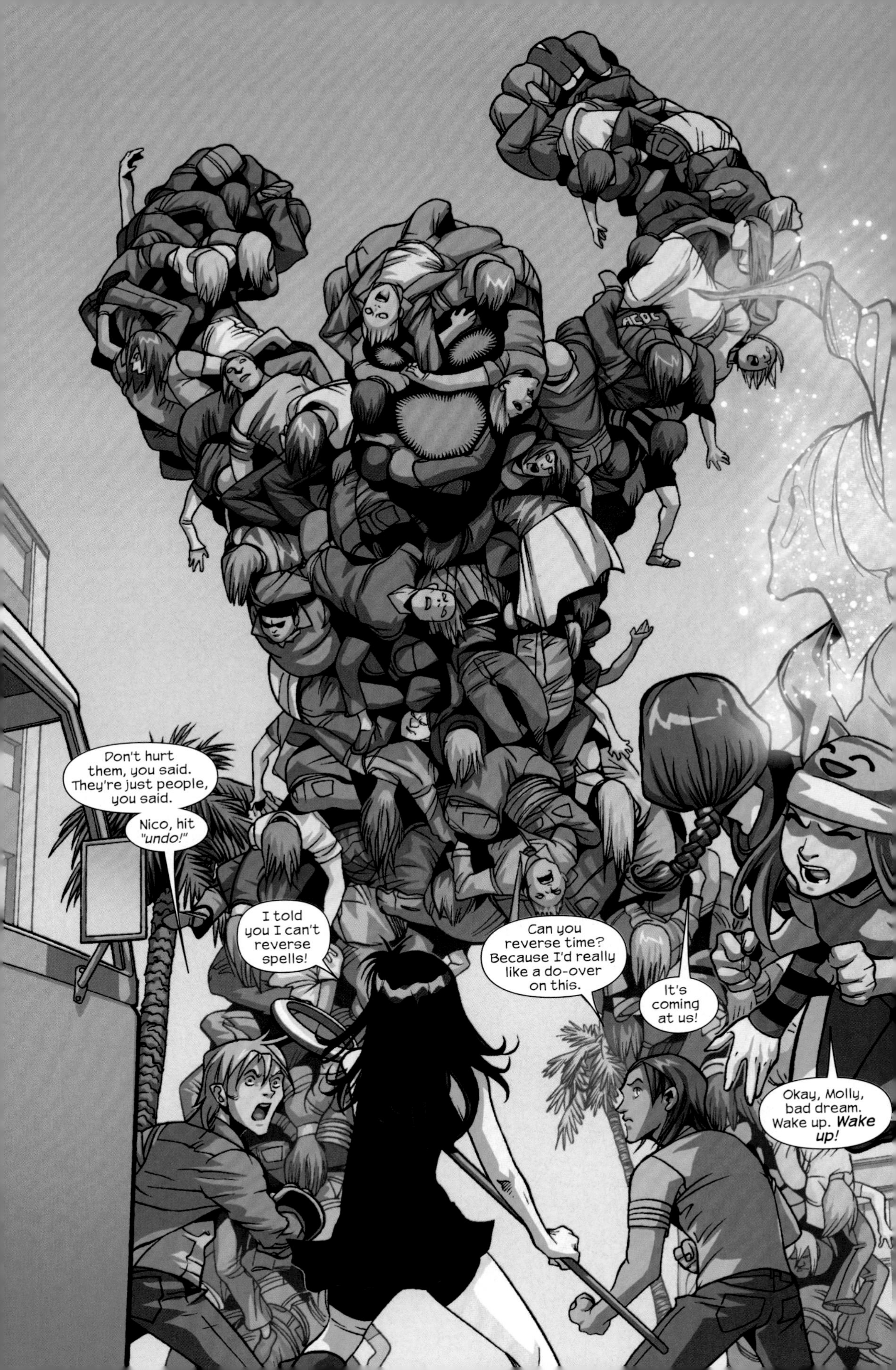
Don't hurt them, you said. They're just people, you said.
Nico, hit "undo!"
I told you I can't reverse spells!
Can you reverse time? Because I'd really like a do-over on this.
It's coming at us!
Okay, Molly, bad dream. Wake up. Wake up!

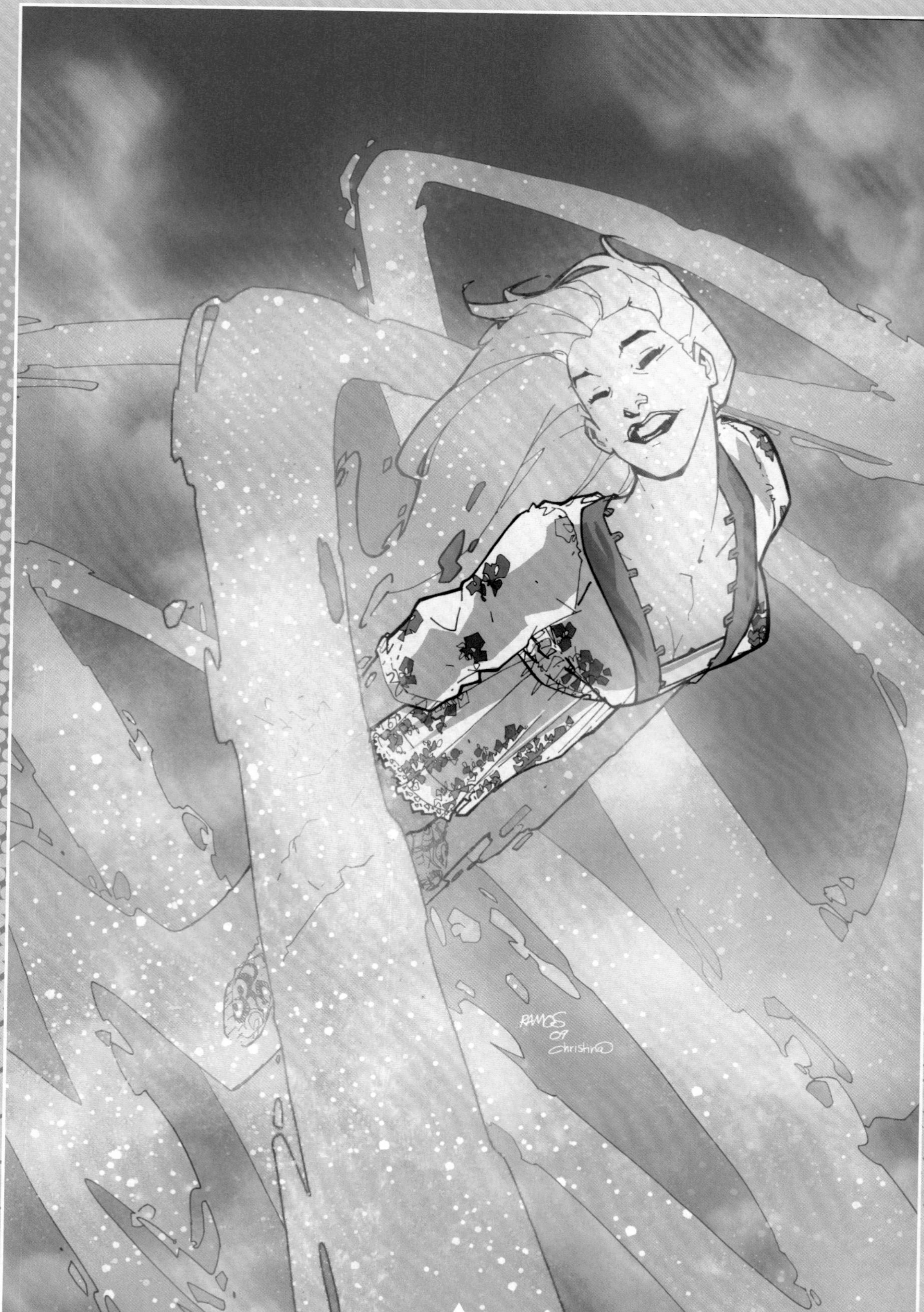
RAMOS
09
christina

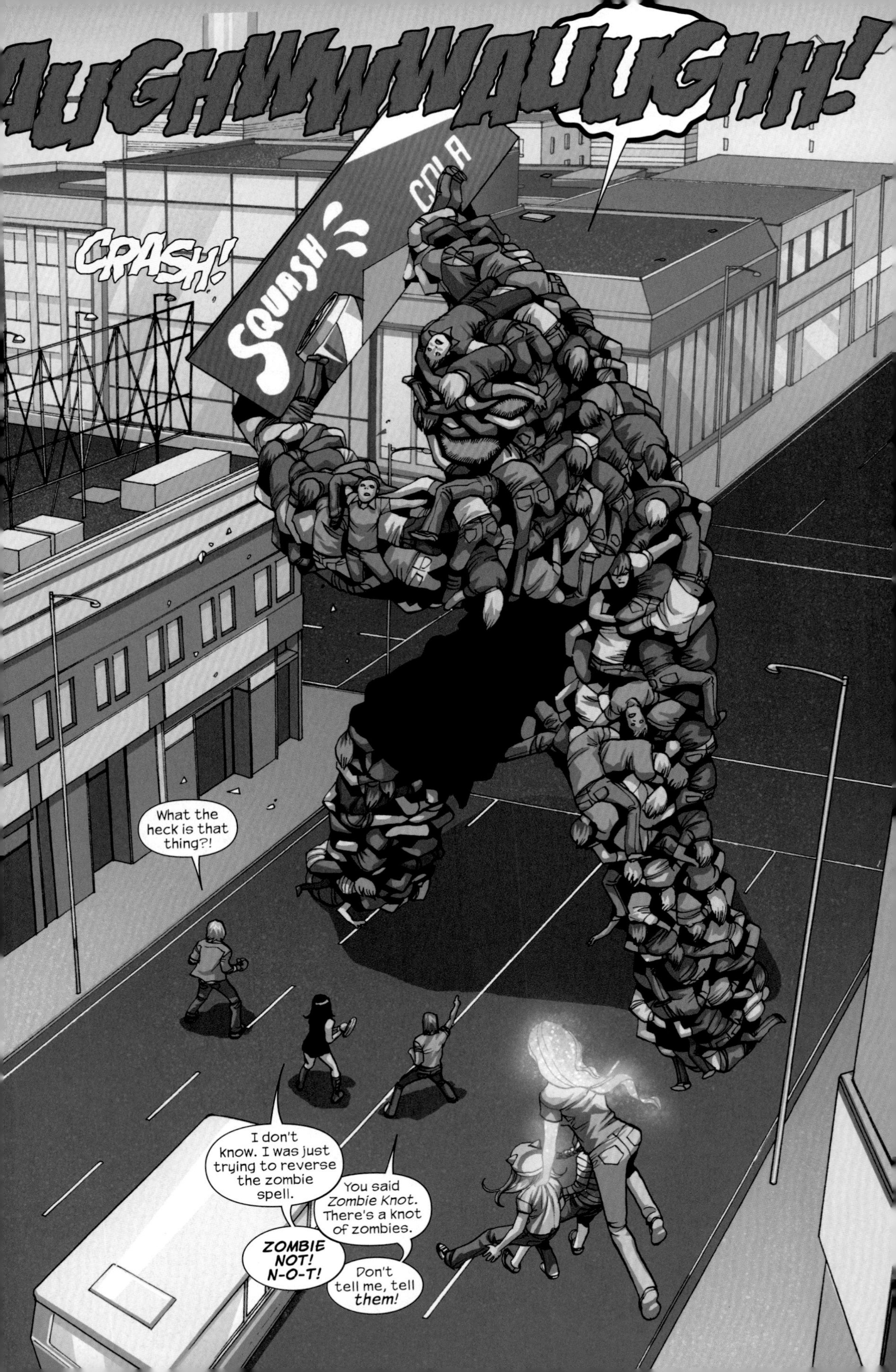
AUGHWWWAUUUGHH!
CRASH!
SQUASH COLA
What the heck is that thing?!
I don't know. I was just trying to reverse the zombie spell.
You said *Zombie Knot*. There's a knot of zombies.
ZOMBIE NOT! N-O-T!
Don't tell me, tell ***them!***

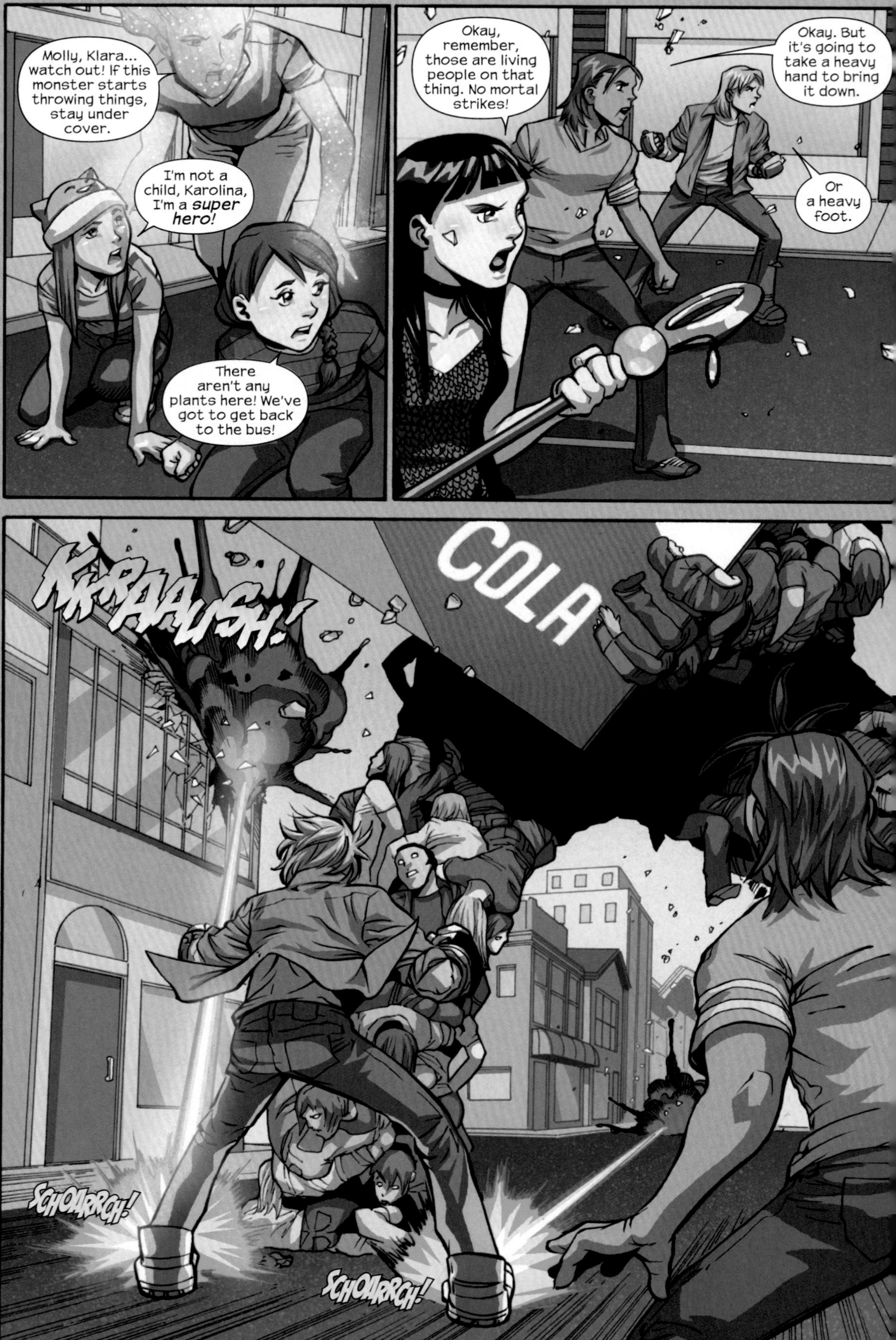
Molly, Klara... watch out! If this monster starts throwing things, stay under cover.
I'm not a child, Karolina, I'm a *super hero!*
There aren't any plants here! We've got to get back to the bus!
Okay, remember, those are living people on that thing. No mortal strikes!
Okay. But it's going to take a heavy hand to bring it down.
Or a heavy foot.
KRRAAUSH!
COLA
SCHOARRCH!
SCHOARRCH!

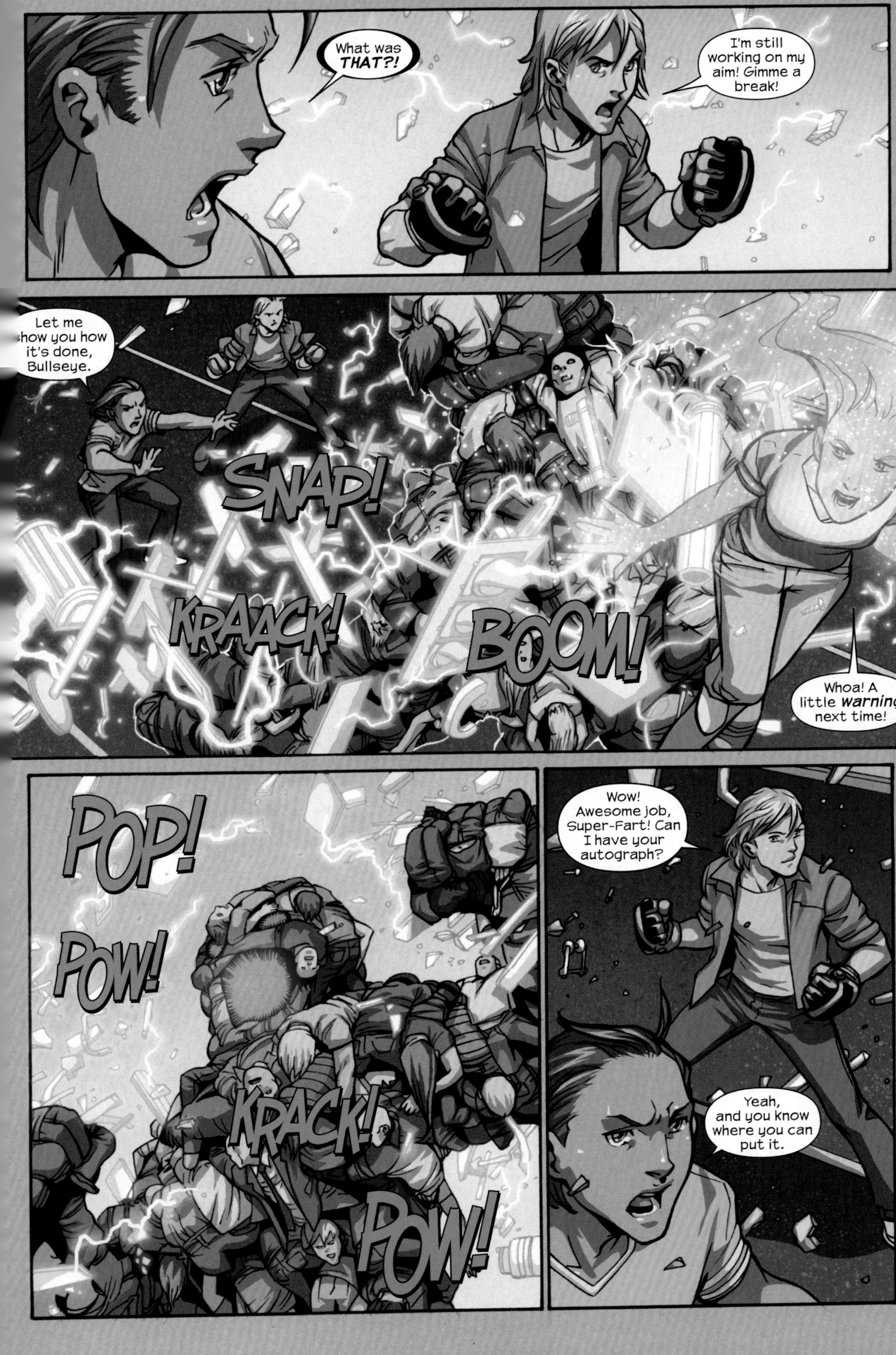
What was **THAT?!**
I'm still working on my aim! Gimme a break!
Let me show you how it's done, Bullseye.
SNAP!
KRAACK!
BOOM!
Whoa! A little **warning** next time!
POP!
POW!
KRACK!
POW!
Wow! Awesome job, Super-Fart! Can I have your autograph?
Yeah, and you know where you can put it.

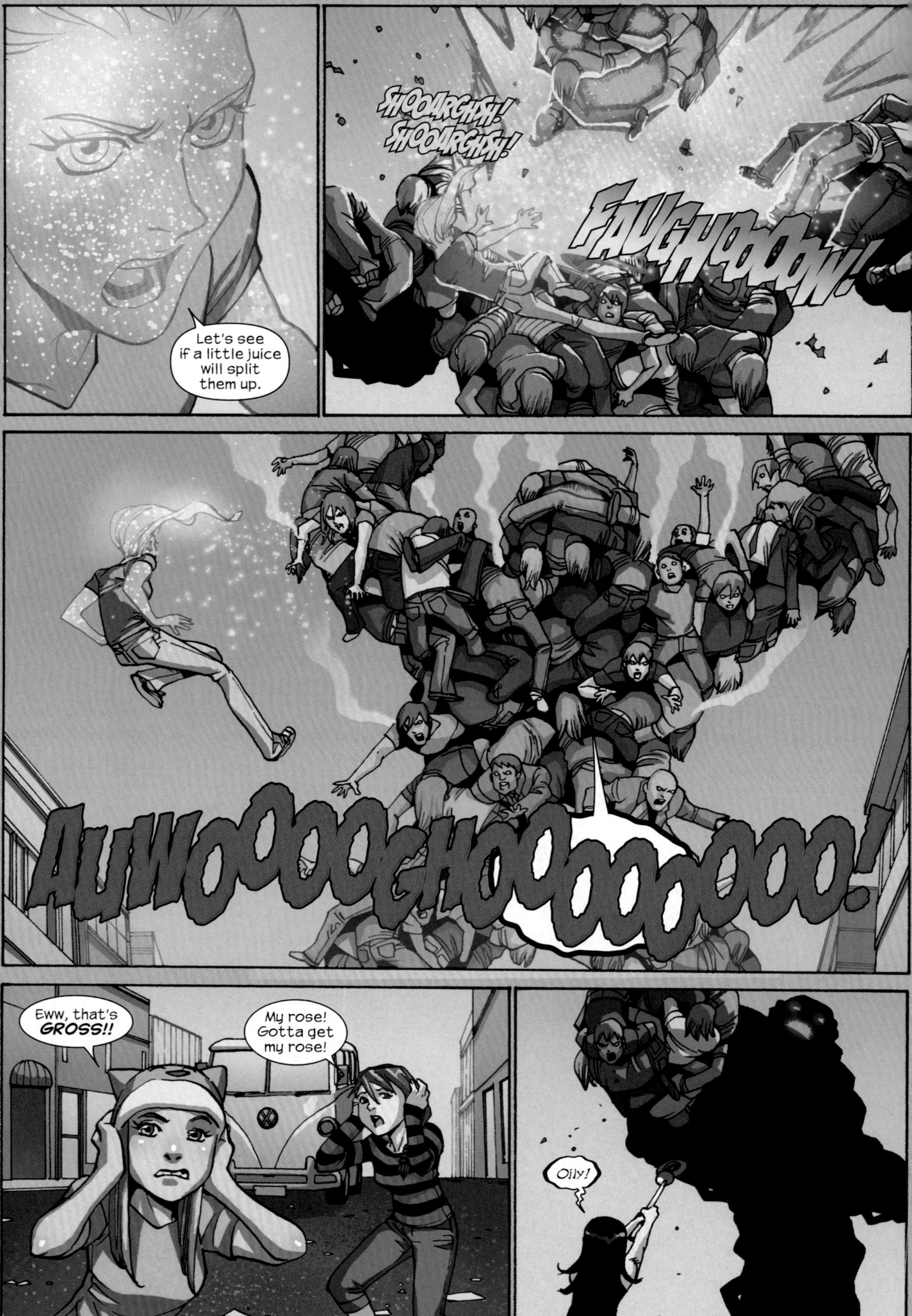
Let's see if a little juice will split them up.
SHOOARGHSH! SHOOARGHSH!
FAUGHOOOOW!
AUWOOOOGHOOOOOOOO!
Eww, that's GROSS!!
My rose! Gotta get my rose!
Oilly!

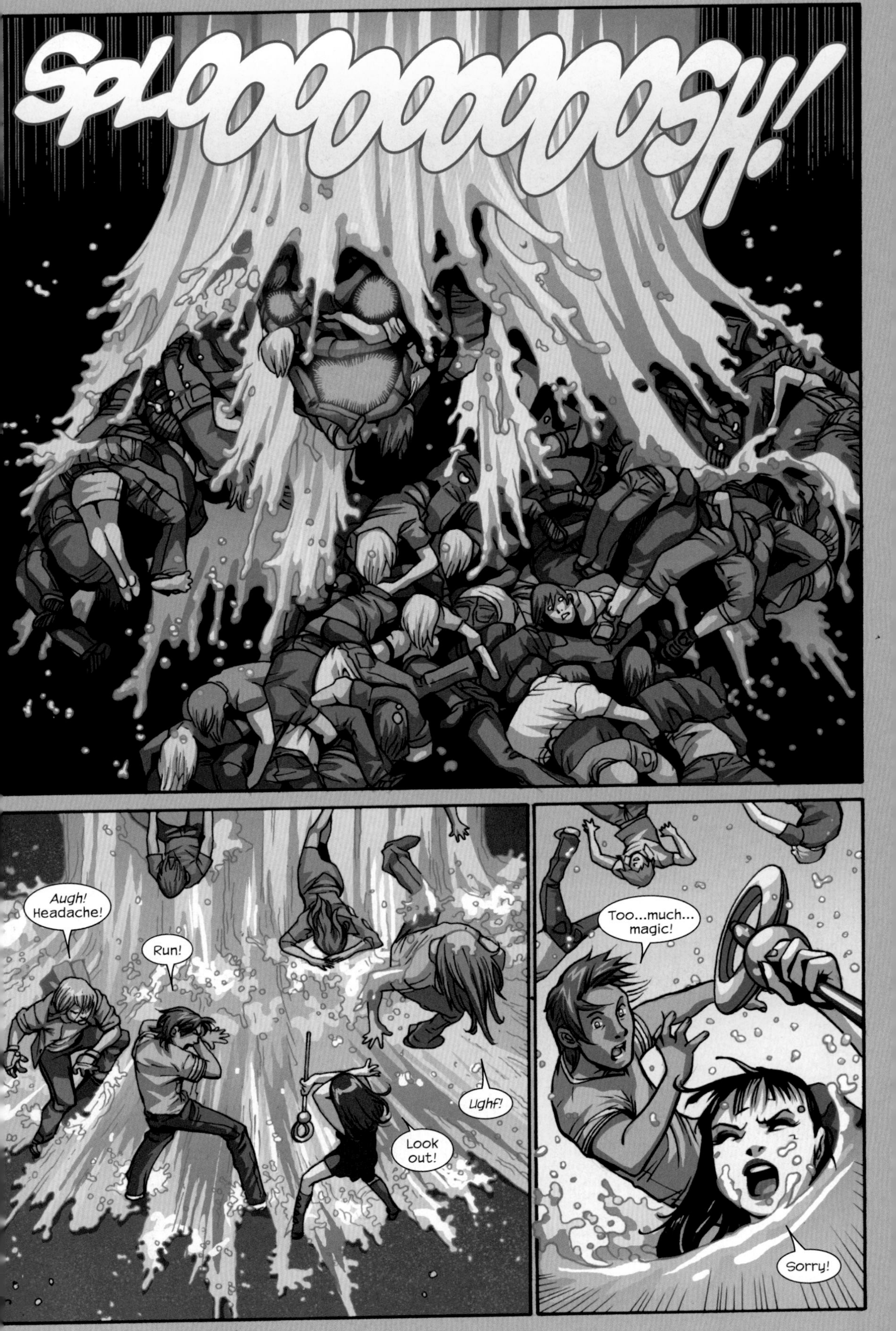
SPLOOOOOOOOOSH!
Augh! Headache!
Run!
Look out!
Ughf!
Too...much... magic!
Sorry!

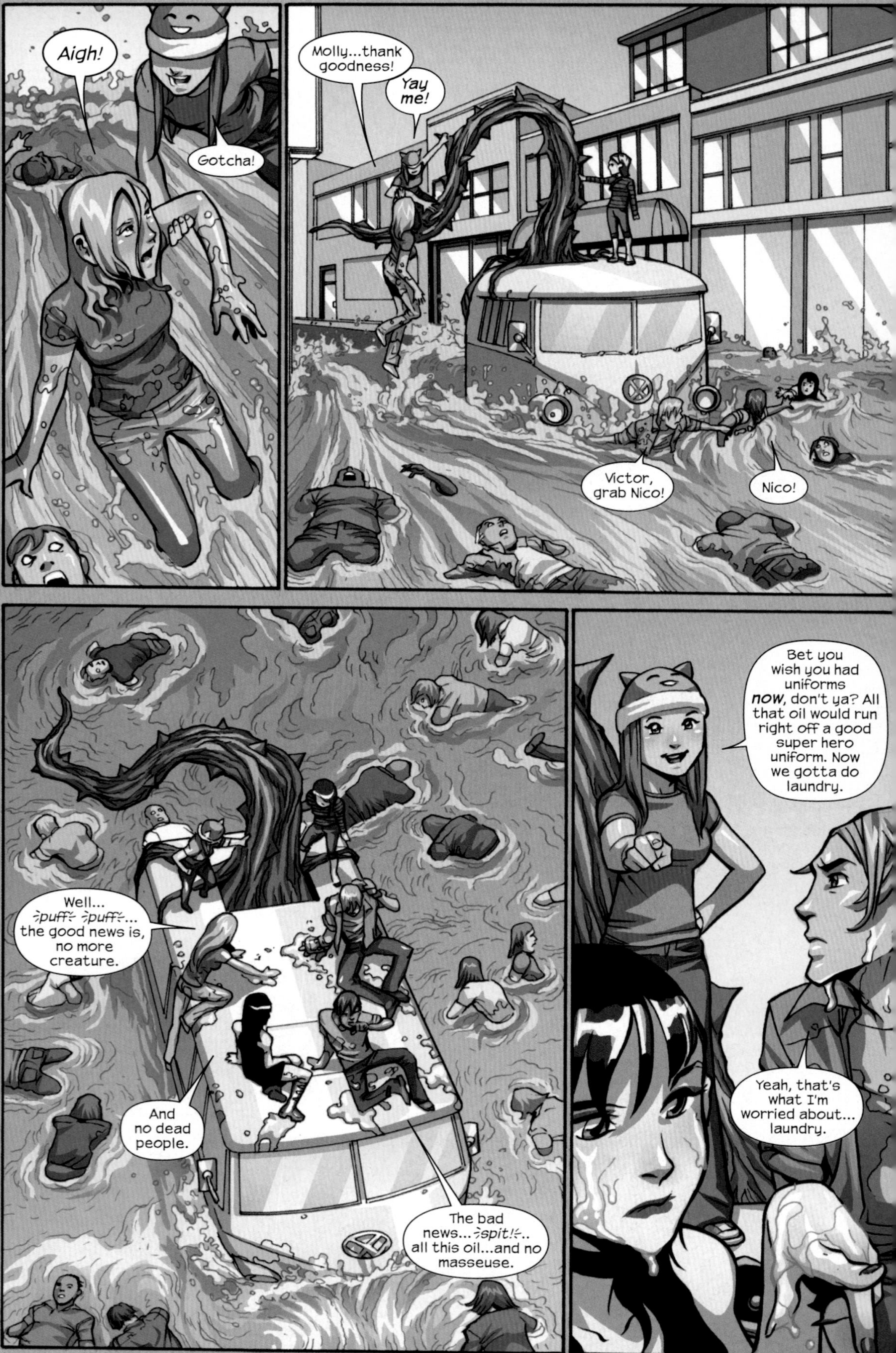
Aigh!
Gotcha!
Molly...thank goodness!
Yay me!
Victor, grab Nico!
Nico!
Well... ≷puff≶ ≷puff≶... the good news is, no more creature.
And no dead people.
The bad news... ≷spit!≶.. all this oil...and no masseuse.
Bet you wish you had uniforms NOW, don't ya? All that oil would run right off a good super hero uniform. Now we gotta do laundry.
Yeah, that's what I'm worried about... laundry.

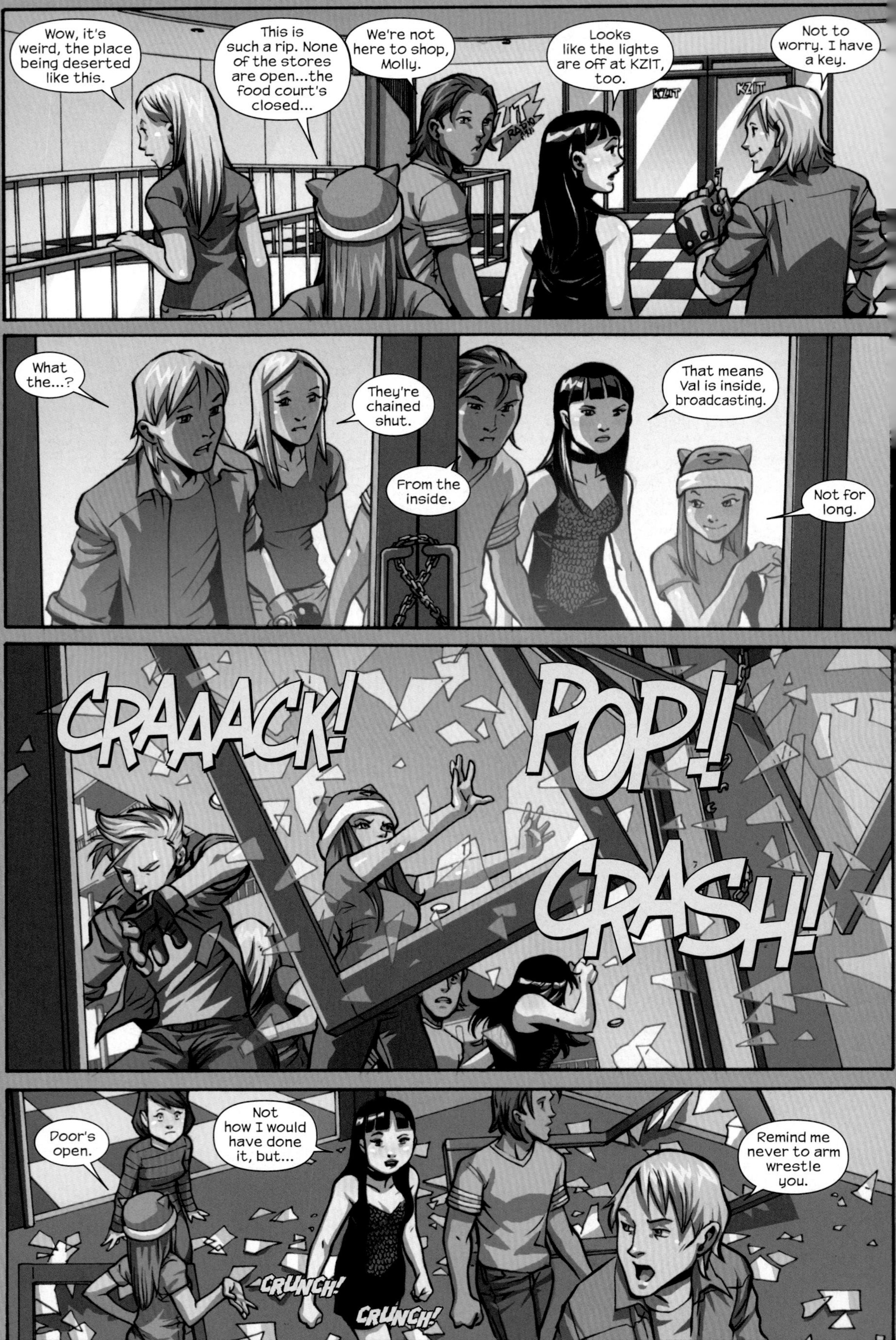
Wow, it's weird, the place being deserted like this.
This is such a rip. None of the stores are open...the food court's closed...
We're not here to shop, Molly.
Looks like the lights are off at KZIT, too.
KZIT
KZIT
Not to worry. I have a key.
What the...?
They're chained shut.
From the inside.
That means Val is inside, broadcasting.
Not for long.
CRAAACK!
POP!!
CRASH!
Door's open.
Not how I would have done it, but...
Remind me never to arm wrestle you.
CRUNCH!
CRUNCH!

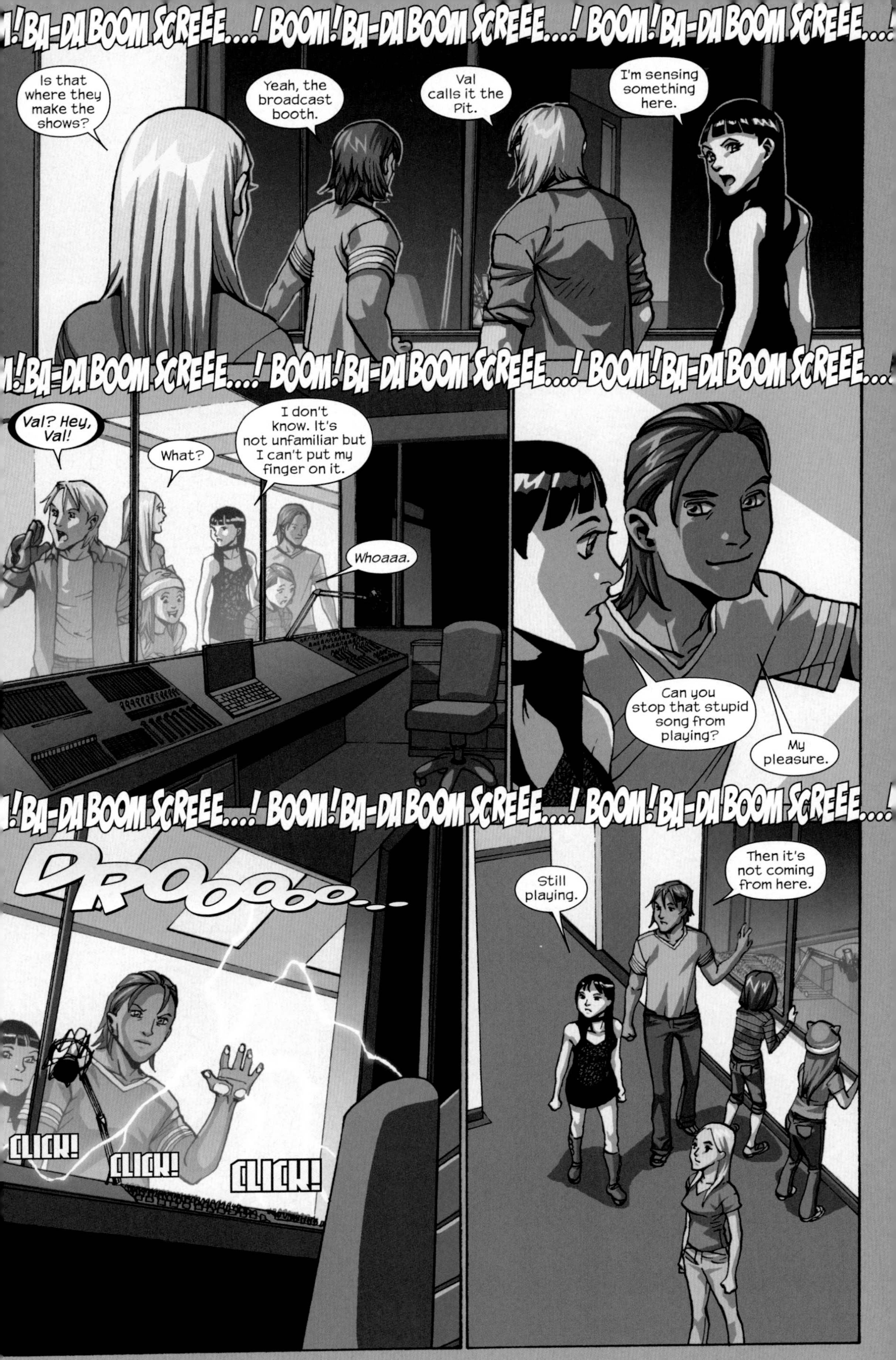

BOOM! BA-DA BOOM SCREEE...! BOOM! BA-DA BOOM SCREEE...! BOOM! BA-DA BOOM SCREEE...!
Is that where they make the shows?
Yeah, the broadcast booth.
Val calls it the Pit.
I'm sensing something here.
BOOM! BA-DA BOOM SCREEE...! BOOM! BA-DA BOOM SCREEE...! BOOM! BA-DA BOOM SCREEE...!
Val? Hey, Val!
What?
I don't know. It's not unfamiliar but I can't put my finger on it.
Whoaaa.
Can you stop that stupid song from playing?
My pleasure.
BOOM! BA-DA BOOM SCREEE...! BOOM! BA-DA BOOM SCREEE...! BOOM! BA-DA BOOM SCREEE...!
DROOOOOOO...
CLICK!
CLICK!
CLICK!
Still playing.
Then it's not coming from here.

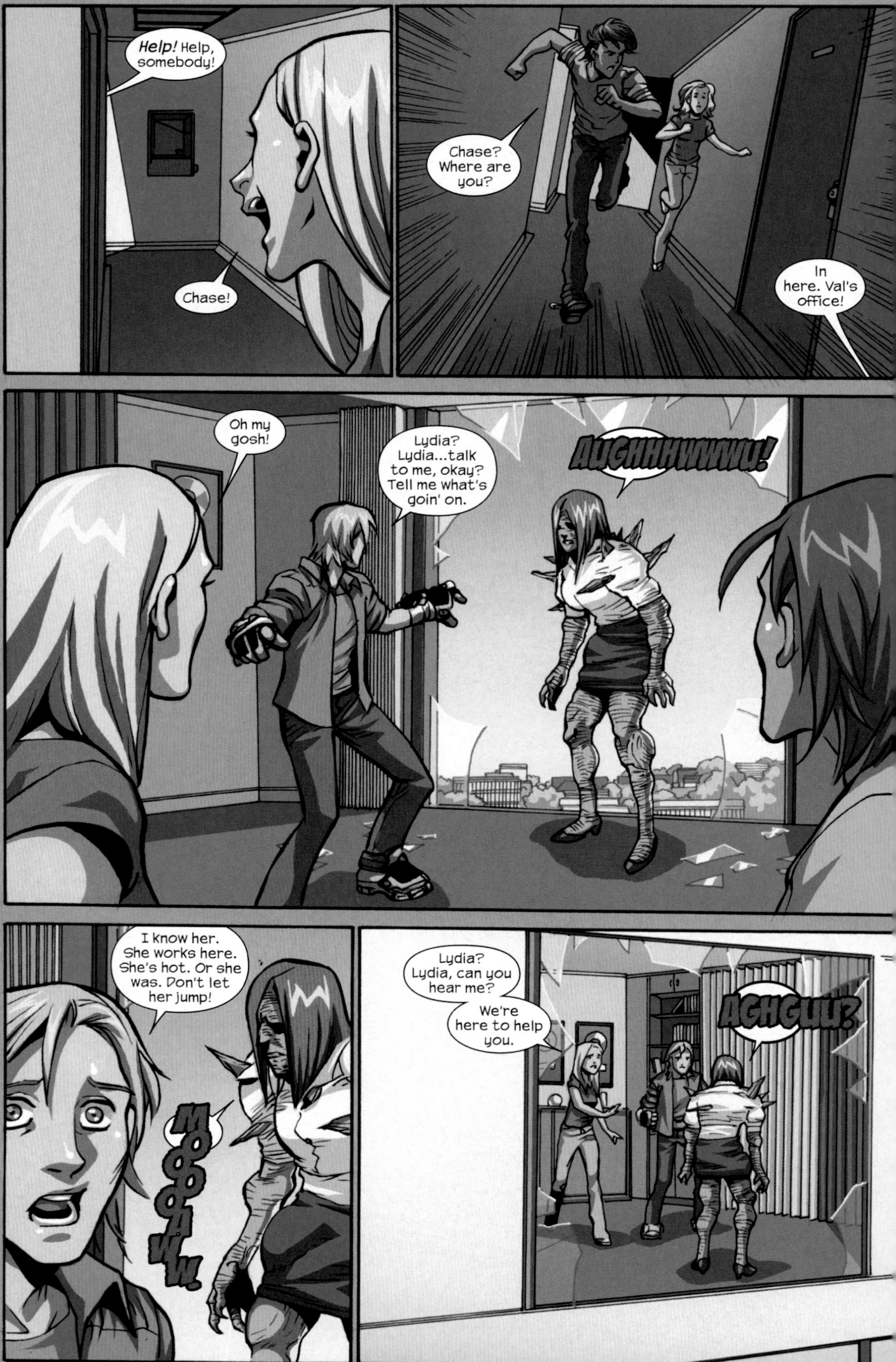
Help! Help, somebody!
Chase!
Chase? Where are you?
In here. Val's office!
Oh my gosh!
Lydia? Lydia...talk to me, okay? Tell me what's goin' on.
AUGHHHWWWU!
I know her. She works here. She's hot. Or she was. Don't let her jump!
MOOOOAWW!
Lydia? Lydia, can you hear me?
We're here to help you.
AGHGUU?

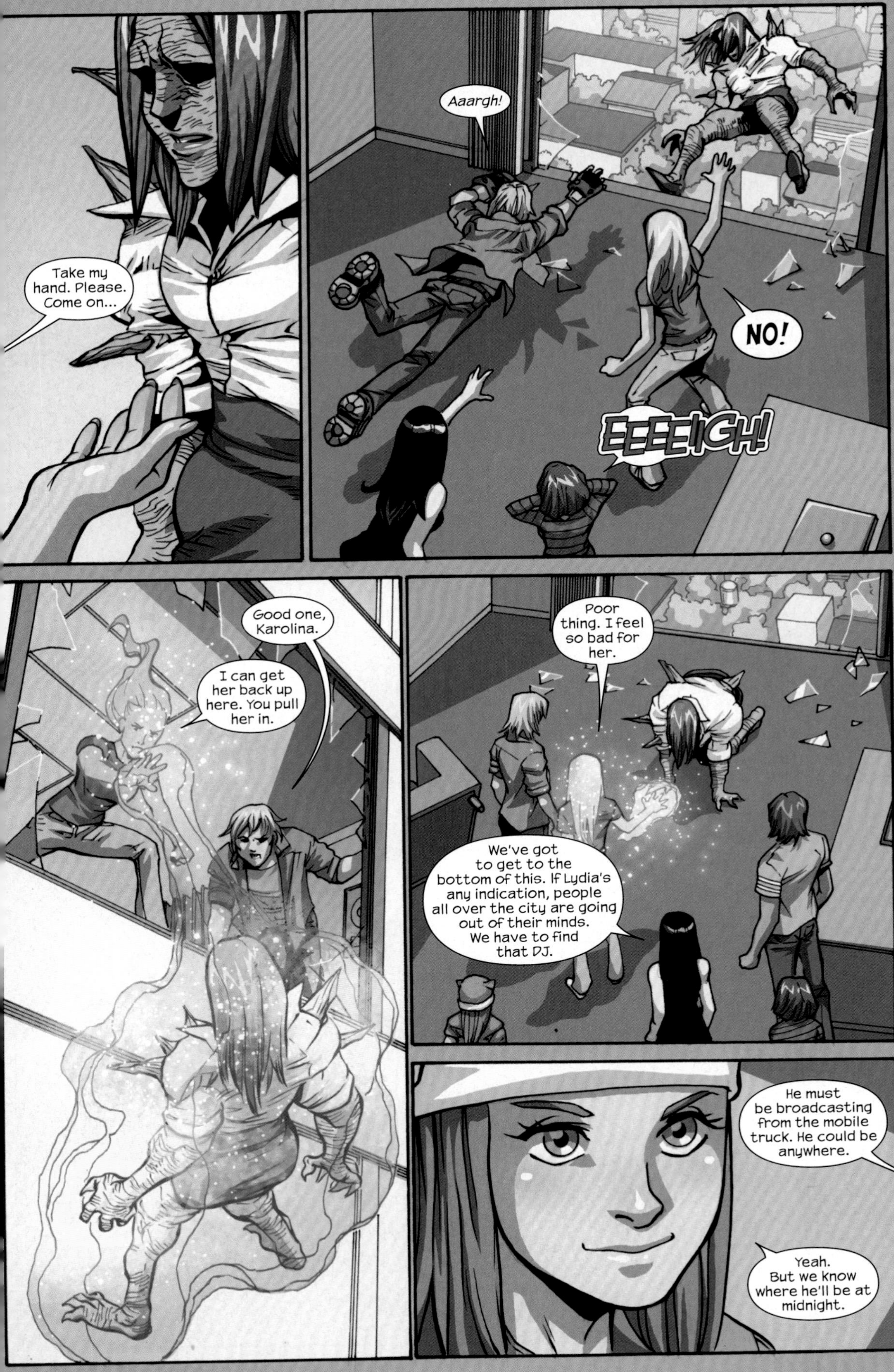
Take my hand. Please. Come on...
Aaargh!
NO!
EEEEIGH!
Good one, Karolina.
I can get her back up here. You pull her in.
Poor thing. I feel so bad for her.
We've got to get to the bottom of this. If Lydia's any indication, people all over the city are going out of their minds. We have to find that DJ.
He must be broadcasting from the mobile truck. He could be anywhere.
Yeah. But we know where he'll be at midnight.

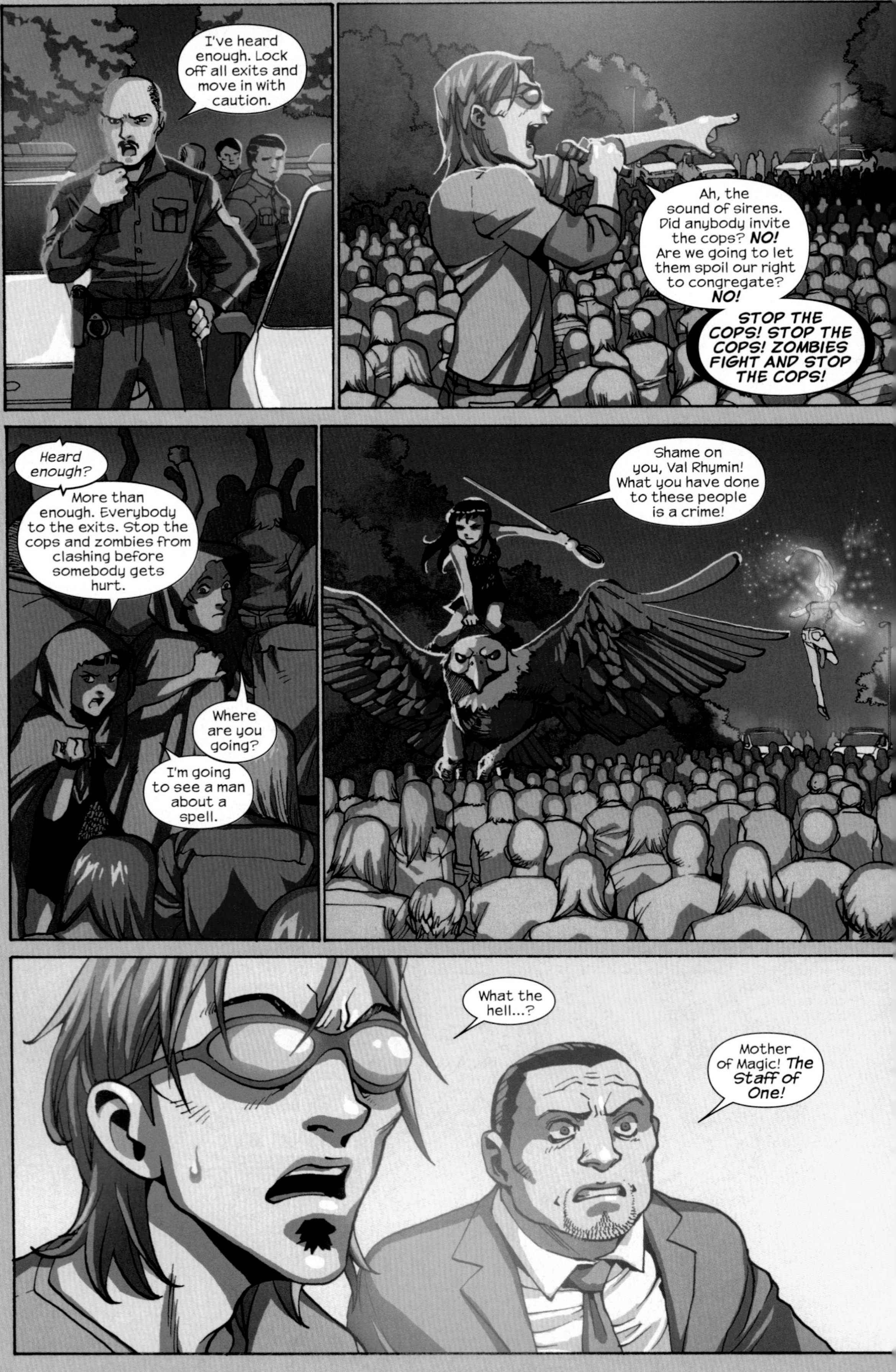
I've heard enough. Lock off all exits and move in with caution.
Ah, the sound of sirens. Did anybody invite the cops? NO! Are we going to let them spoil our right to congregate? NO!
STOP THE COPS! STOP THE COPS! ZOMBIES FIGHT AND STOP THE COPS!
Heard enough?
More than enough. Everybody to the exits. Stop the cops and zombies from clashing before somebody gets hurt.
Where are you going?
I'm going to see a man about a spell.
Shame on you, Val Rhymin! What you have done to these people is a crime!
What the hell...?
Mother of Magic! The Staff of One!

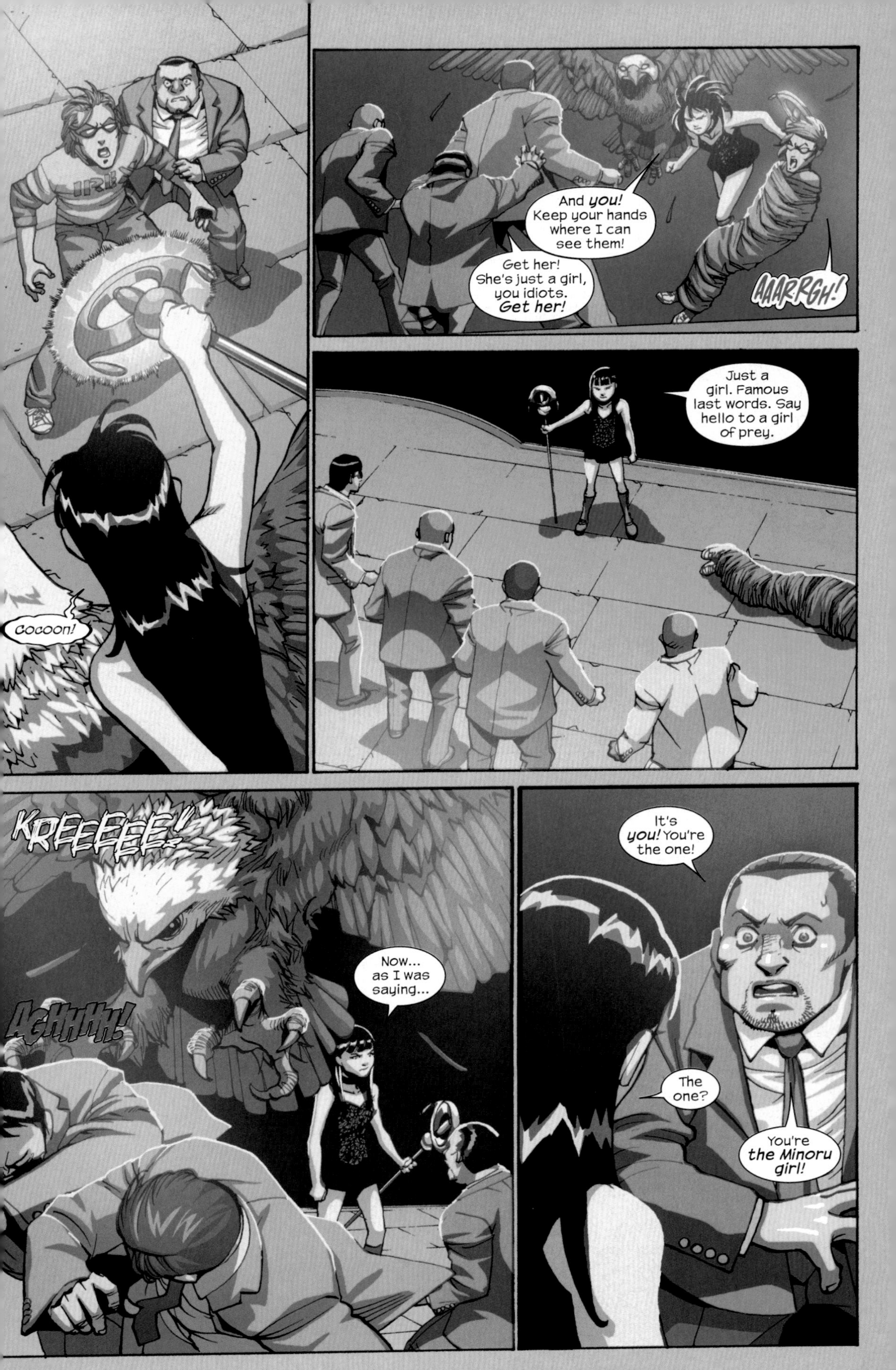
Cocoon!
And you! Keep your hands where I can see them!
Get her! She's just a girl, you idiots. Get her!
AAARRGH!
Just a girl. Famous last words. Say hello to a girl of prey.
KREEEEEE!
AGHHHH!
Now... as I was saying...
It's you! You're the one!
The one?
You're the Minoru girl!

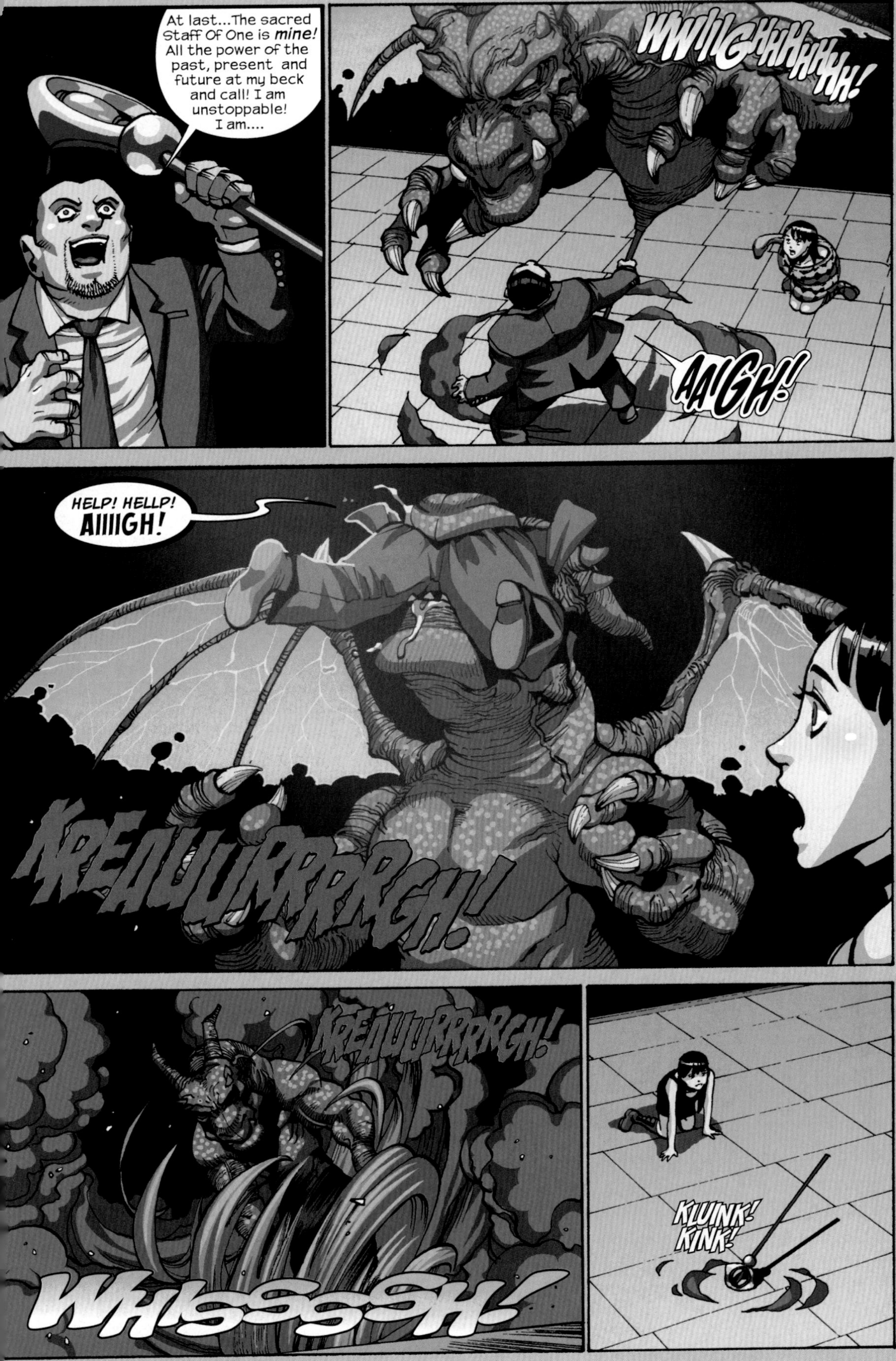

At last...The sacred Staff Of One is *mine!* All the power of the past, present and future at my beck and call! I am unstoppable! I am....
WWIIIGHHHHHHH!
AAUGH!
HELP! HELLP! AIIIIGH!
KREAUURRRRGH!
KREAUURRRRGH!
WHISSSSSH!
KLUINK! KINK!

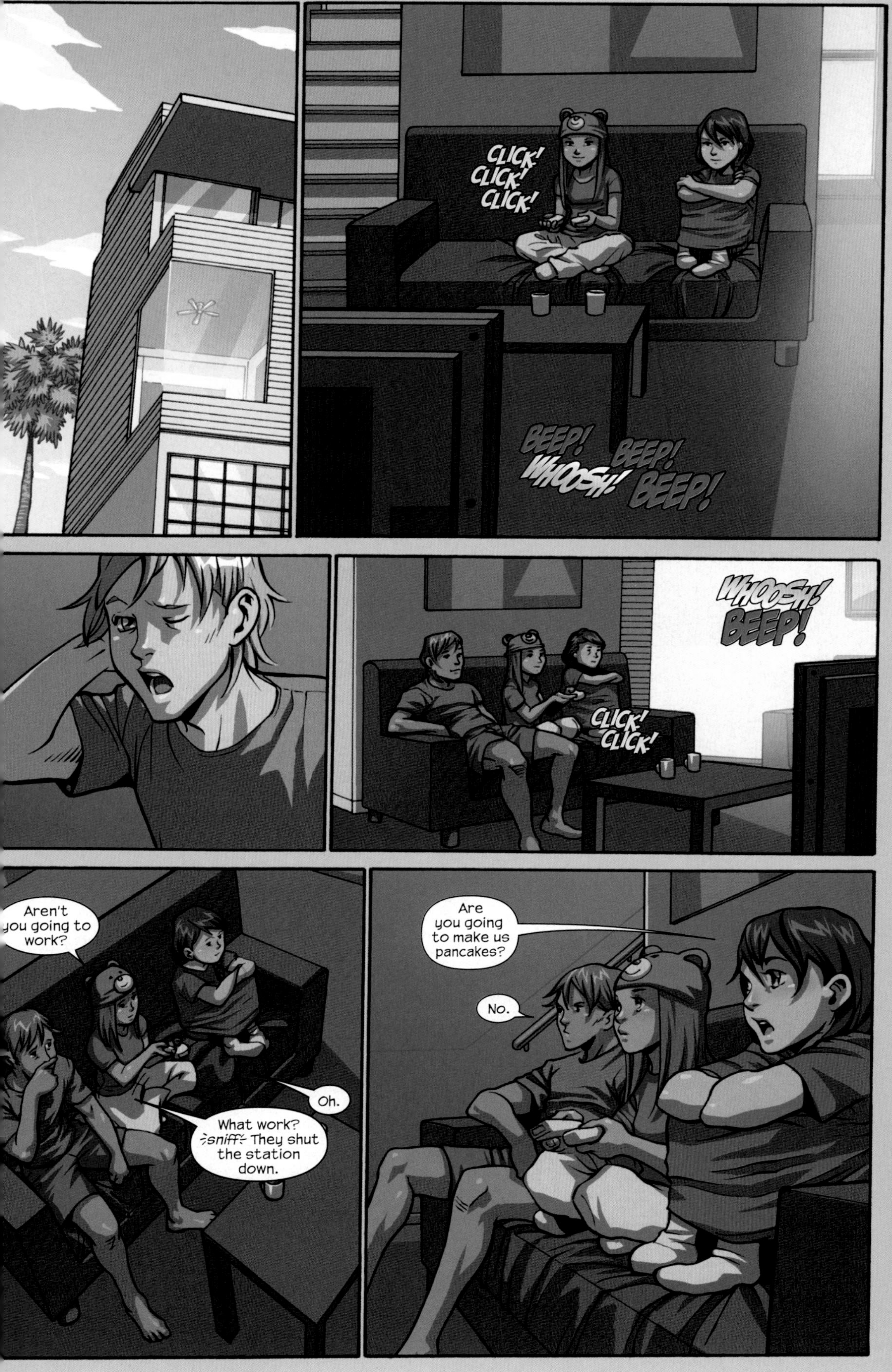
CLICK! CLICK! CLICK!
BEEP! BEEP! WHOOSH! BEEP!
WHOOSH! BEEP!
CLICK! CLICK!
Aren't you going to work?
What work? -sniff- They shut the station down.
Oh.
Are you going to make us pancakes?
No.

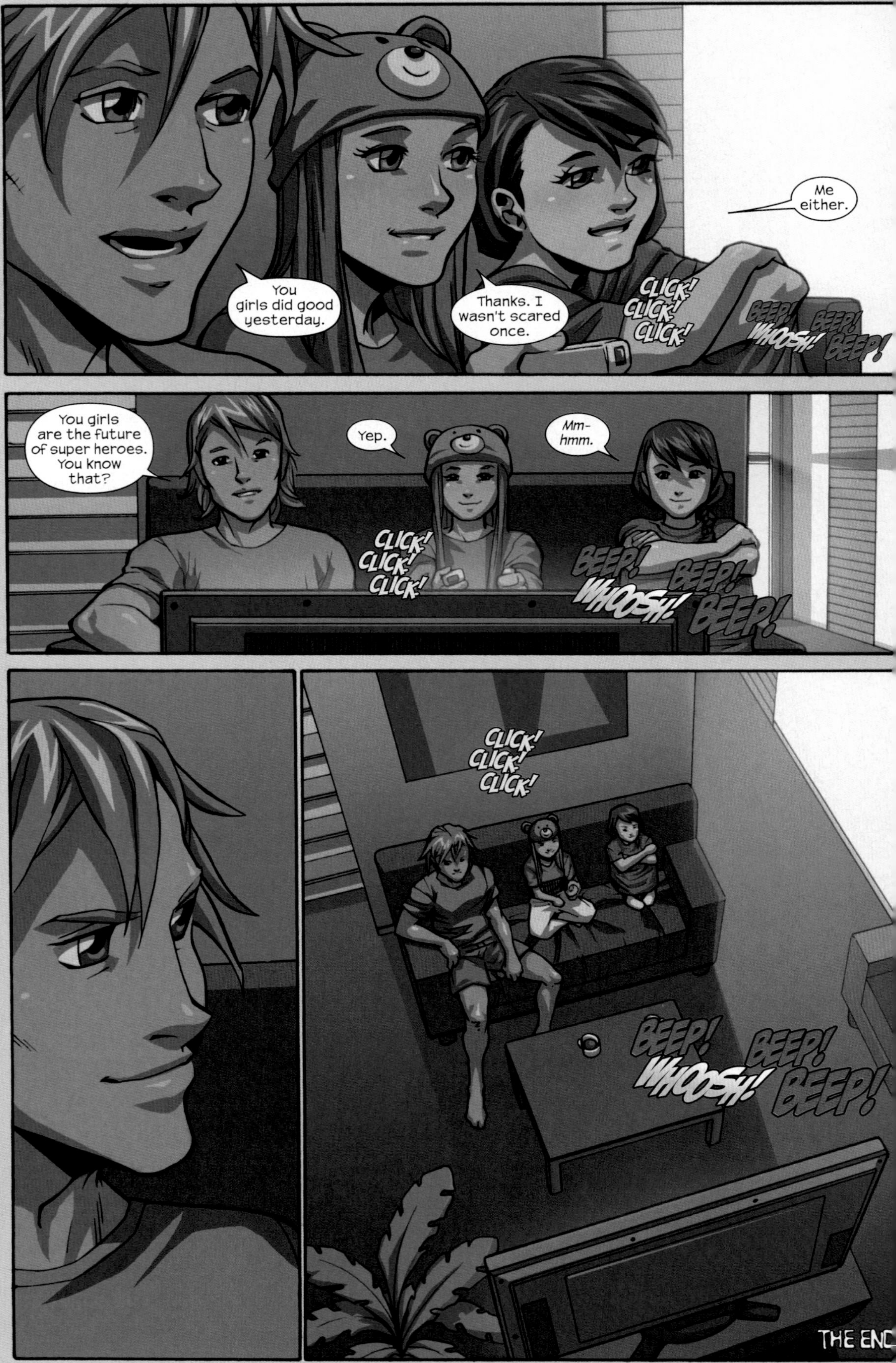
You girls did good yesterday.
Thanks. I wasn't scared once.
Me either.
CLICK! CLICK! CLICK!
BEEP! WHOOSH! BEEP! BEEP!
You girls are the future of super heroes. You know that?
Yep.
Mm-hmm.
CLICK! CLICK! CLICK!
BEEP! WHOOSH! BEEP! BEEP!
CLICK! CLICK! CLICK!
BEEP! WHOOSH! BEEP! BEEP!
THE END

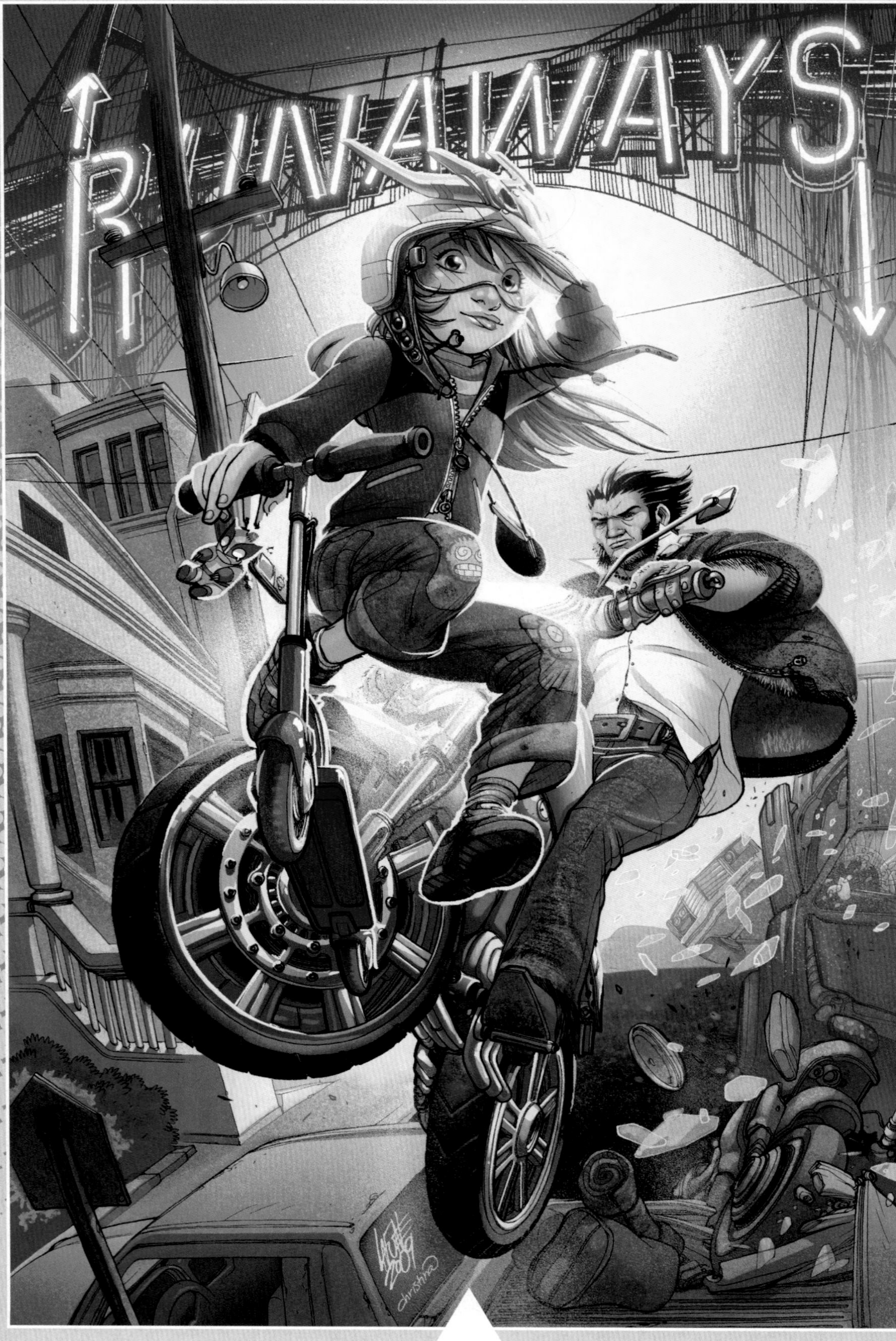
RUNAWAYS

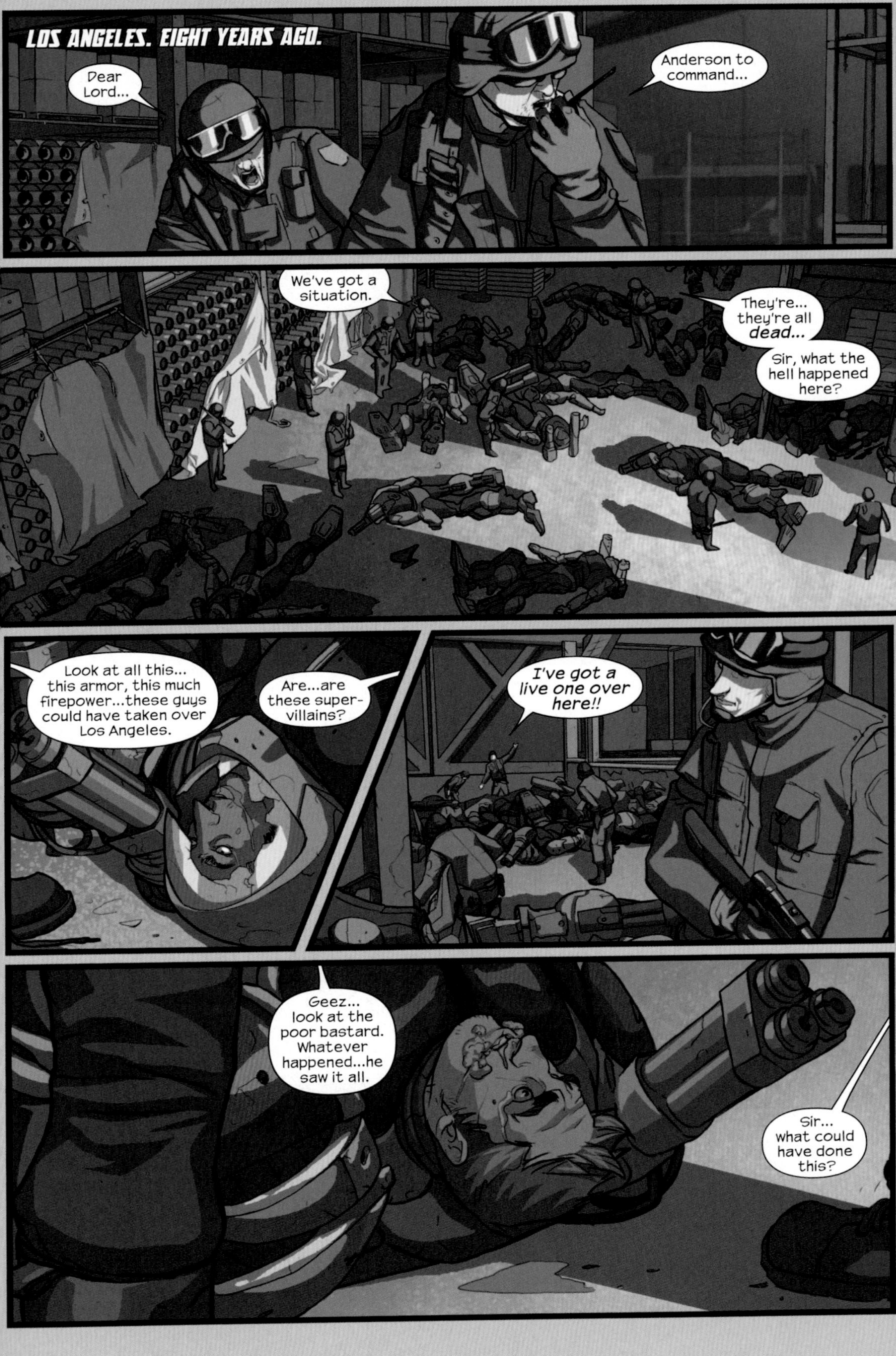
LOS ANGELES. EIGHT YEARS AGO.
Dear Lord...
Anderson to command...
We've got a situation.
They're... they're all *dead...*
Sir, what the hell happened here?
Look at all this... this armor, this much firepower...these guys could have taken over Los Angeles.
Are...are these super-villains?
I've got a live one over here!!
Geez... look at the poor bastard. Whatever happened...he saw it all.
Sir... what could have done this?

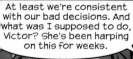
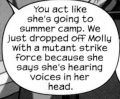

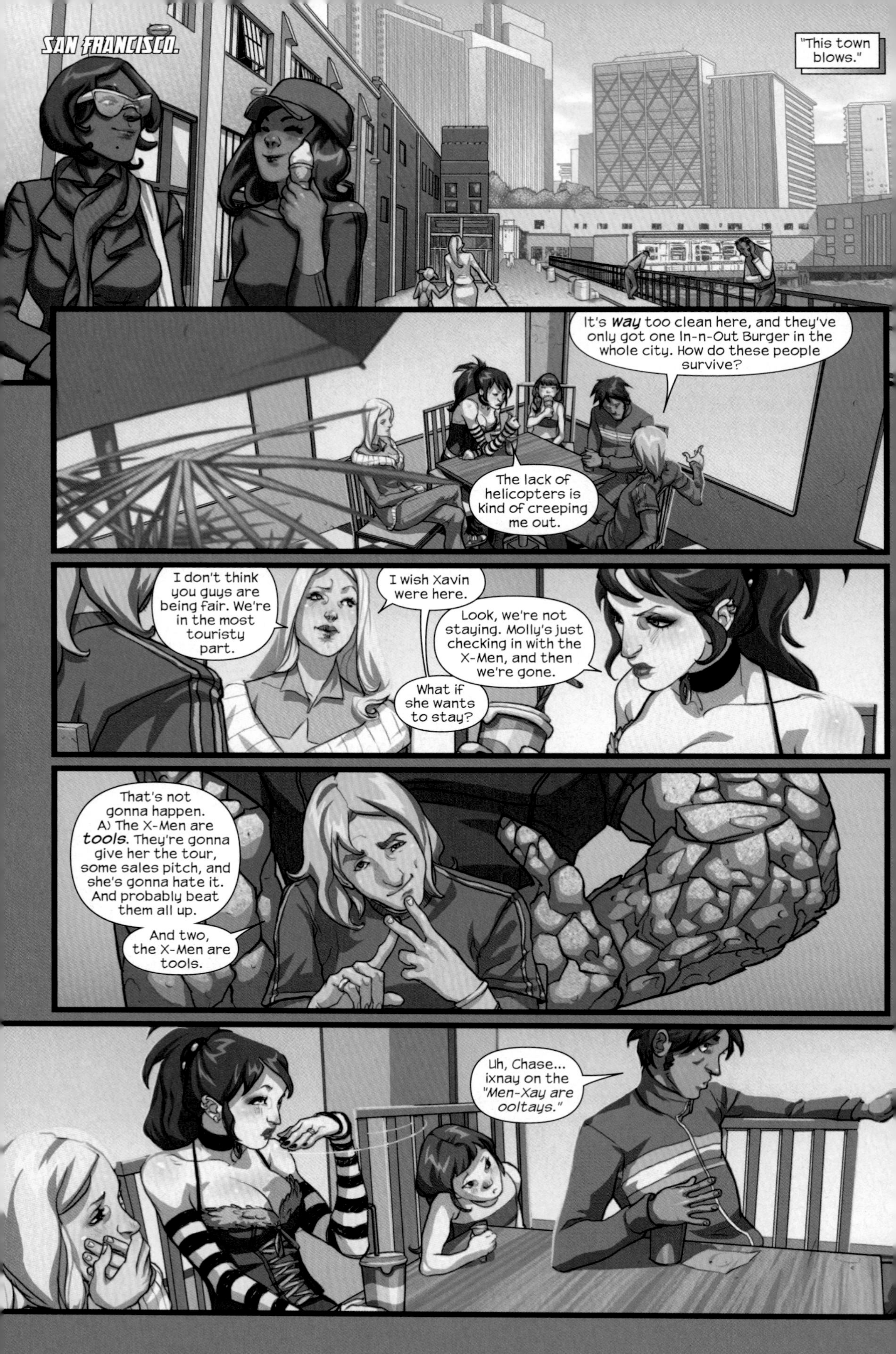
SAN FRANCISCO.
"This town blows."
It's *way* too clean here, and they've only got one In-n-Out Burger in the whole city. How do these people survive?
The lack of helicopters is kind of creeping me out.
I don't think you guys are being fair. We're in the most touristy part.
I wish Xavin were here.
Look, we're not staying. Molly's just checking in with the X-Men, and then we're gone.
What if she wants to stay?
That's not gonna happen. A) The X-Men are *tools*. They're gonna give her the tour, some sales pitch, and she's gonna hate it. And probably beat them all up.
And two, the X-Men are tools.
Uh, Chase... ixnay on the *"Men-Xay are ooltays."*

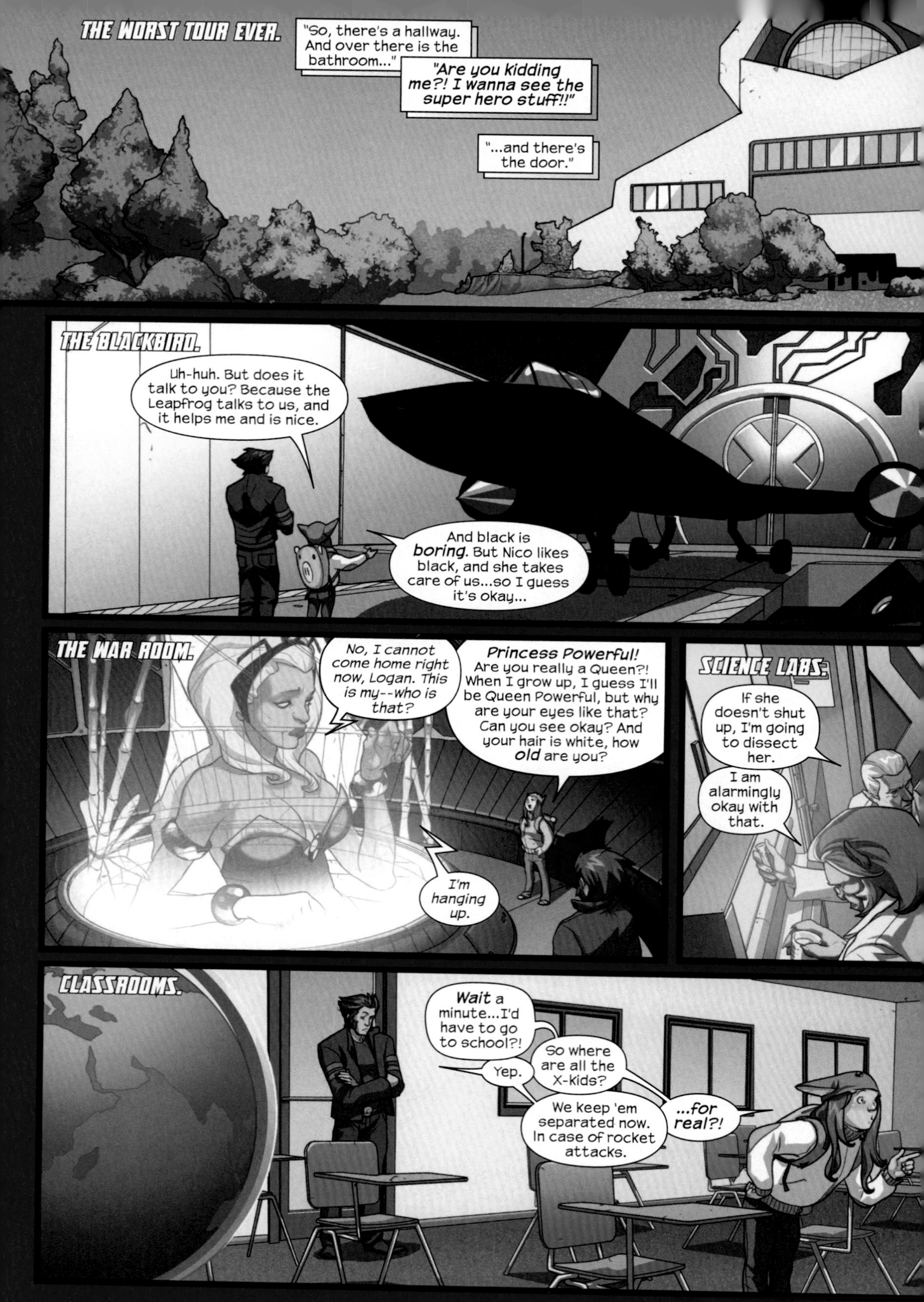
THE WORST TOUR EVER.
"So, there's a hallway. And over there is the bathroom..."
"Are you kidding me?! I wanna see the super hero stuff!!"
"...and there's the door."
THE BLACKBIRD.
Uh-huh. But does it talk to you? Because the Leapfrog talks to us, and it helps me and is nice.
And black is boring. But Nico likes black, and she takes care of us...so I guess it's okay...
THE WAR ROOM.
No, I cannot come home right now, Logan. This is my--who is that?
Princess Powerful! Are you really a Queen?! When I grow up, I guess I'll be Queen Powerful, but why are your eyes like that? Can you see okay? And your hair is white, how old are you?
I'm hanging up.
SCIENCE LABS.
If she doesn't shut up, I'm going to dissect her.
I am alarmingly okay with that.
CLASSROOMS.
Wait a minute...I'd have to go to school?!
Yep.
So where are all the X-kids?
We keep 'em separated now. In case of rocket attacks.
...for real?!

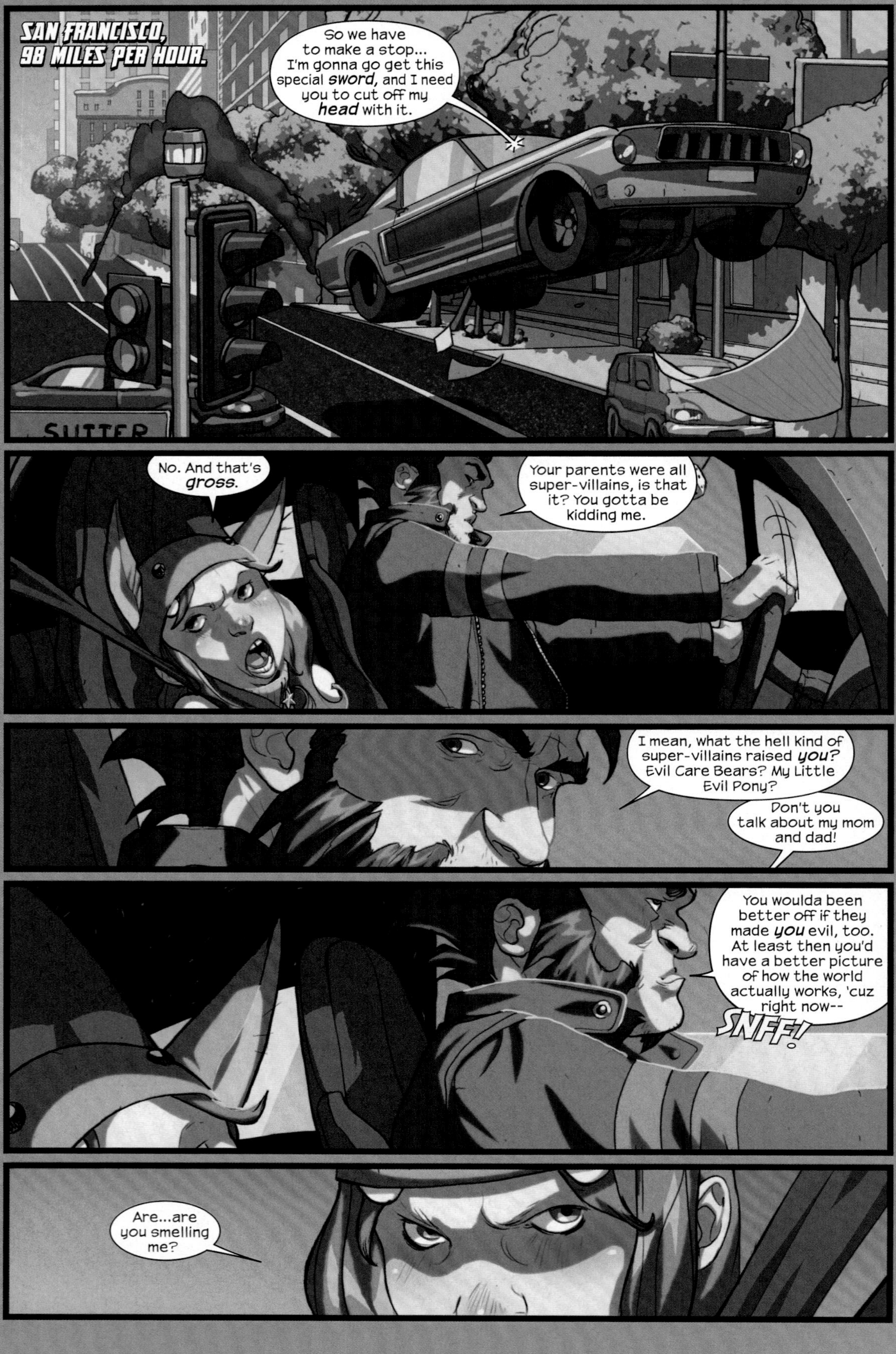
SAN FRANCISCO, 98 MILES PER HOUR.
So we have to make a stop... I'm gonna go get this special sword, and I need you to cut off my head with it.
SUTTER
No. And that's gross.
Your parents were all super-villains, is that it? You gotta be kidding me.
I mean, what the hell kind of super-villains raised you? Evil Care Bears? My Little Evil Pony?
Don't you talk about my mom and dad!
You woulda been better off if they made you evil, too. At least then you'd have a better picture of how the world actually works, 'cuz right now--
SNFF!
Are...are you smelling me?

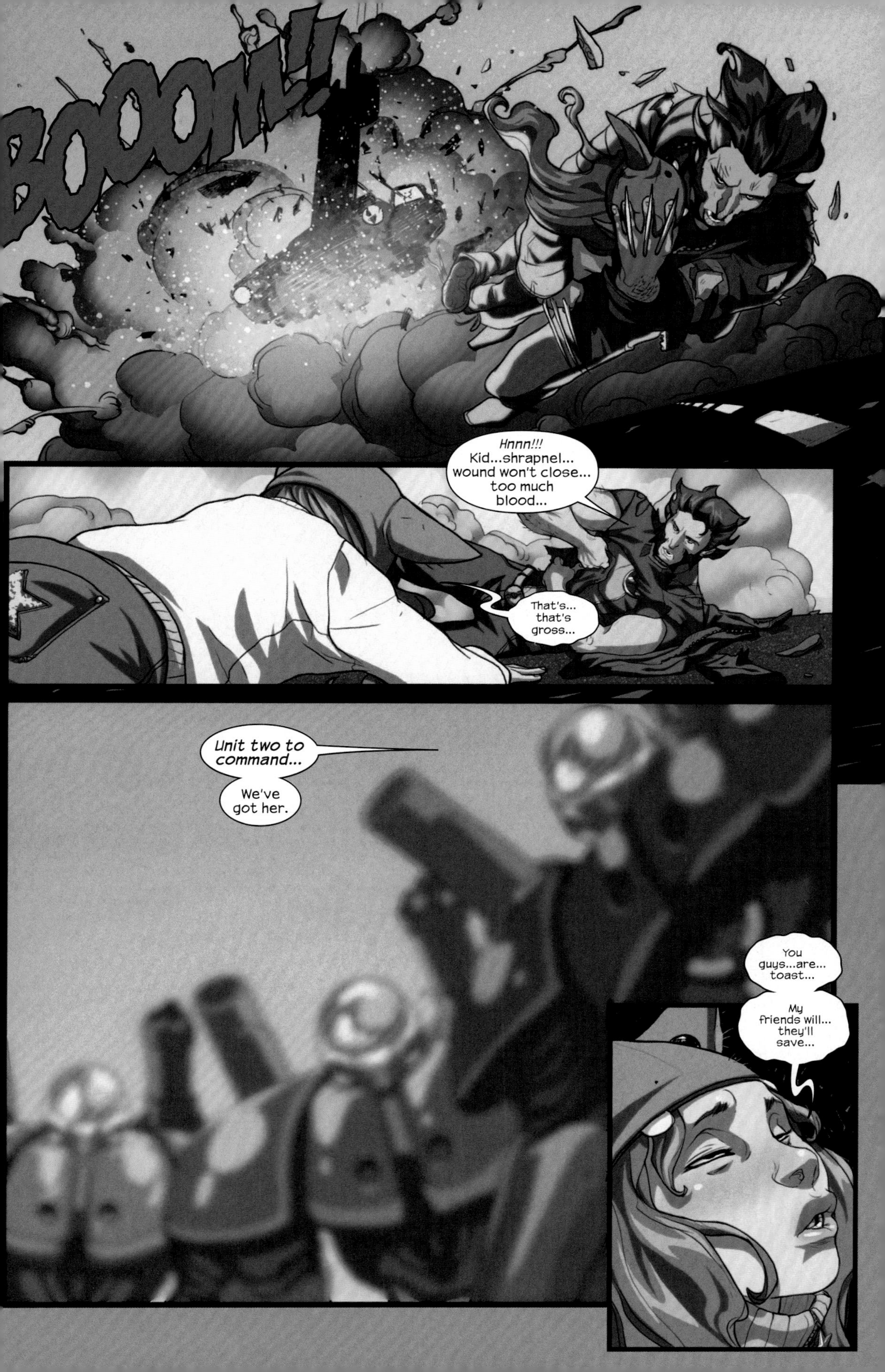
BOOOM!!!
Hnnn!!!
Kid...shrapnel... wound won't close... too much blood...
That's... that's gross...
Unit two to command...
We've got her.
You guys...are... toast...
My friends will... they'll save...

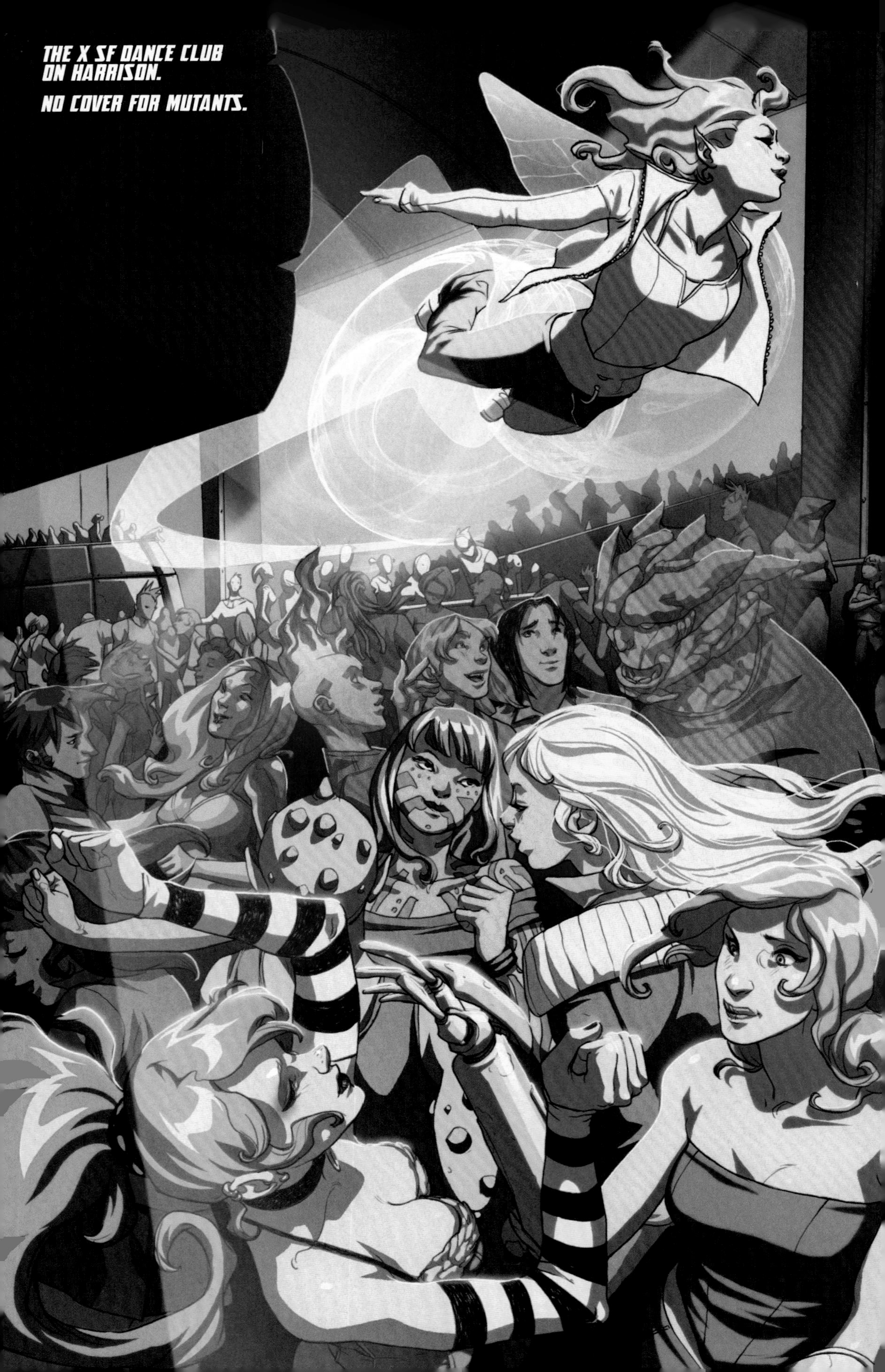
THE X SF DANCE CLUB ON HARRISON.
NO COVER FOR MUTANTS.

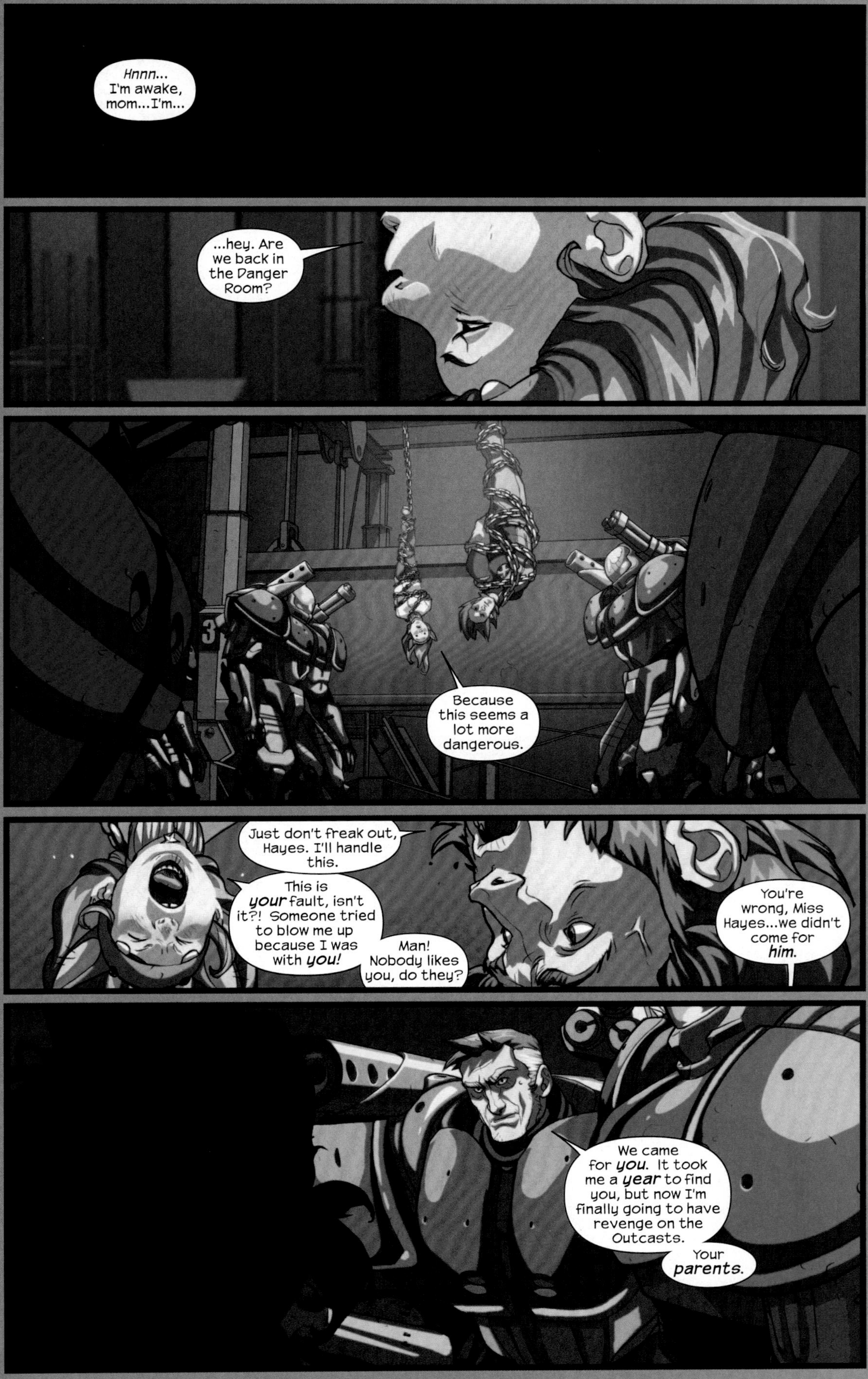

Hnnn... I'm awake, mom...I'm...
...hey. Are we back in the Danger Room?
Because this seems a lot more dangerous.
Just don't freak out, Hayes. I'll handle this.
This is ***your*** fault, isn't it?! Someone tried to blow me up because I was with ***you!***
Man! Nobody likes you, do they?
You're wrong, Miss Hayes...we didn't come for ***him***.
We came for ***you***. It took me a ***year*** to find you, but now I'm finally going to have revenge on the Outcasts.
Your ***parents***.

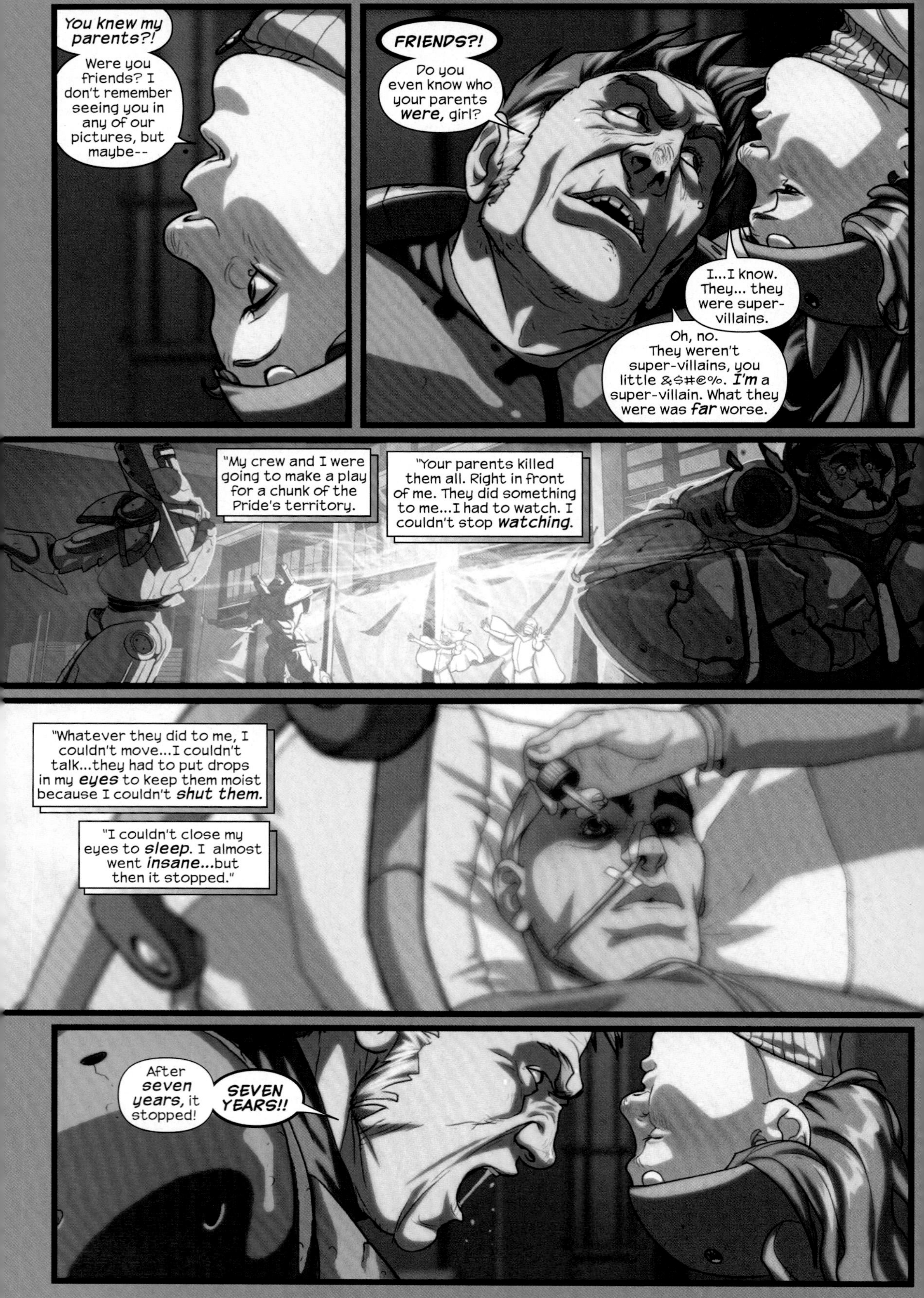
You knew my parents?!
Were you friends? I don't remember seeing you in any of our pictures, but maybe--
FRIENDS?!
Do you even know who your parents were, girl?
I...I know. They... they were super-villains.
Oh, no. They weren't super-villains, you little &$#@%. I'm a super-villain. What they were was far worse.
"My crew and I were going to make a play for a chunk of the Pride's territory.
"Your parents killed them all. Right in front of me. They did something to me...I had to watch. I couldn't stop watching.
"Whatever they did to me, I couldn't move...I couldn't talk...they had to put drops in my eyes to keep them moist because I couldn't shut them.
"I couldn't close my eyes to sleep. I almost went insane...but then it stopped."
After seven years, it stopped!
SEVEN YEARS!!

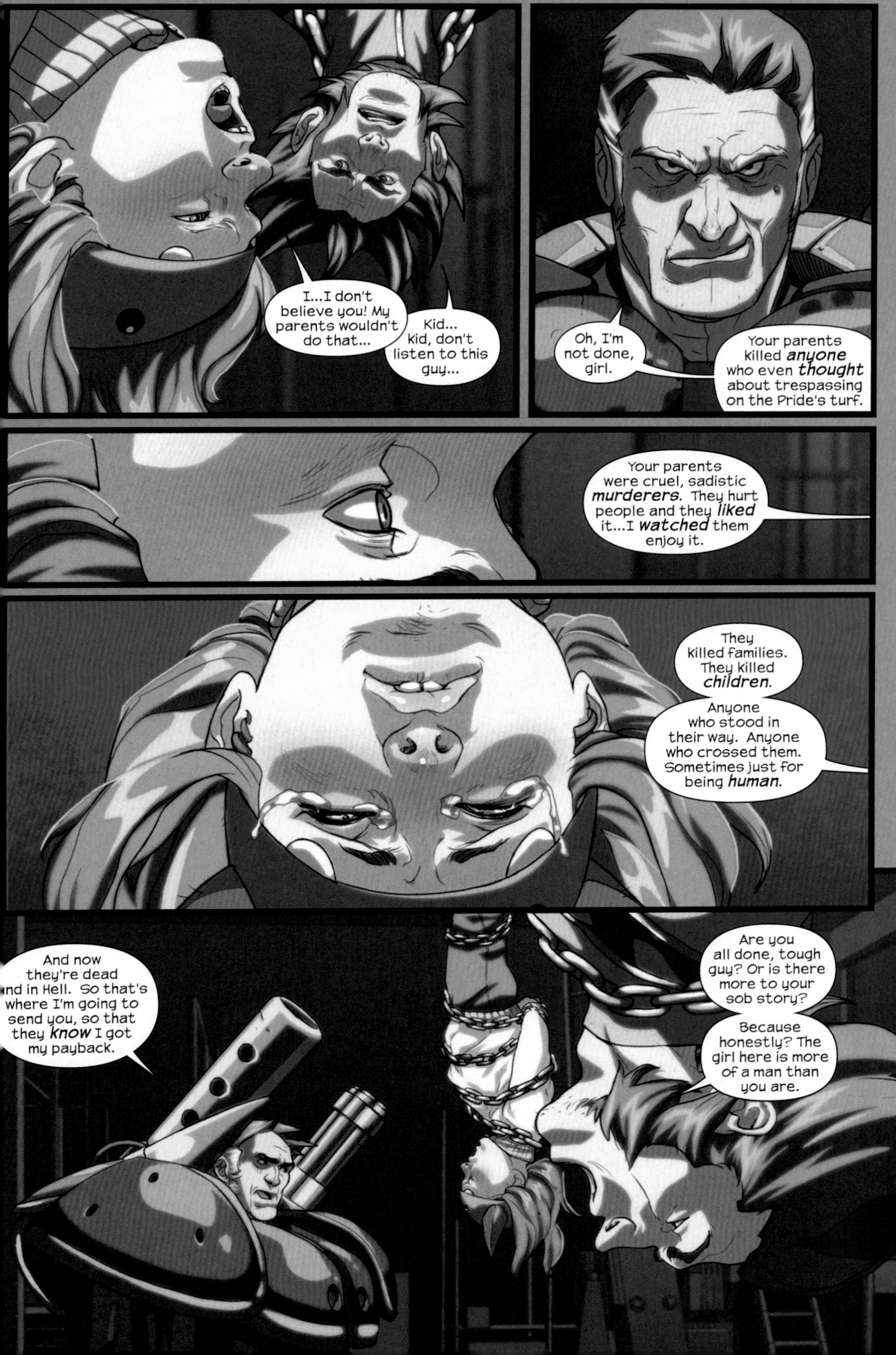

I...I don't believe you! My parents wouldn't do that...
Kid... kid, don't listen to this guy...
Oh, I'm not done, girl.
Your parents killed *anyone* who even *thought* about trespassing on the Pride's turf.
Your parents were cruel, sadistic *murderers*. They hurt people and they *liked* it...I *watched* them enjoy it.
They killed families. They killed *children*.
Anyone who stood in their way. Anyone who crossed them. Sometimes just for being *human*.
And now they're dead nd in Hell. So that's where I'm going to send you, so that they *know* I got my payback.
Are you all done, tough guy? Or is there more to your sob story?
Because honestly? The girl here is more of a man than you are.

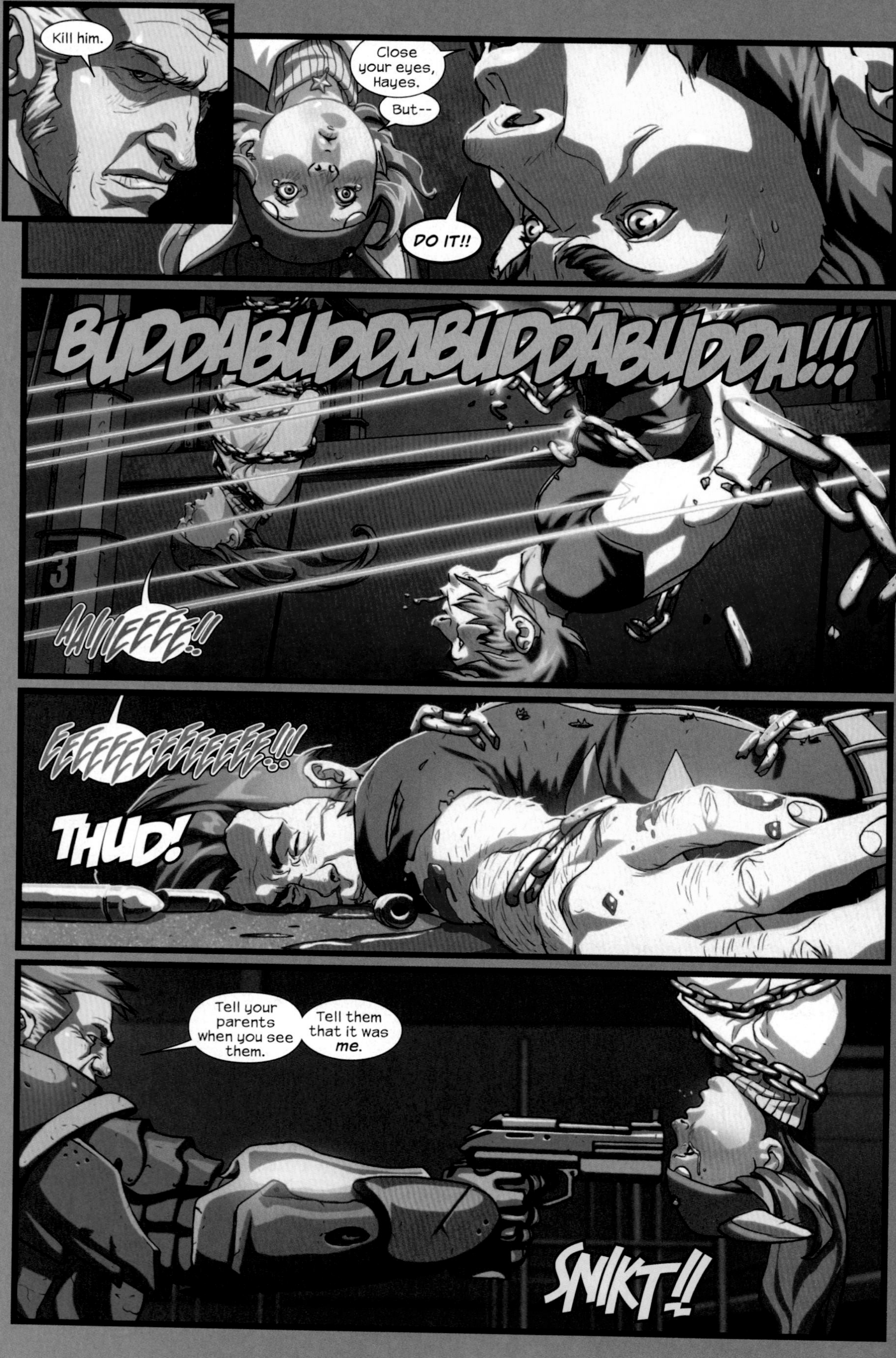
Kill him.
Close your eyes, Hayes.
But--
DO IT!!
BUDDABUDDABUDDABUDDA!!!
AAIIIEEEE!!
EEEEEEEEEEEEEE!!!
THUD!
Tell your parents when you see them.
Tell them that it was *me*.
SNIKT!!

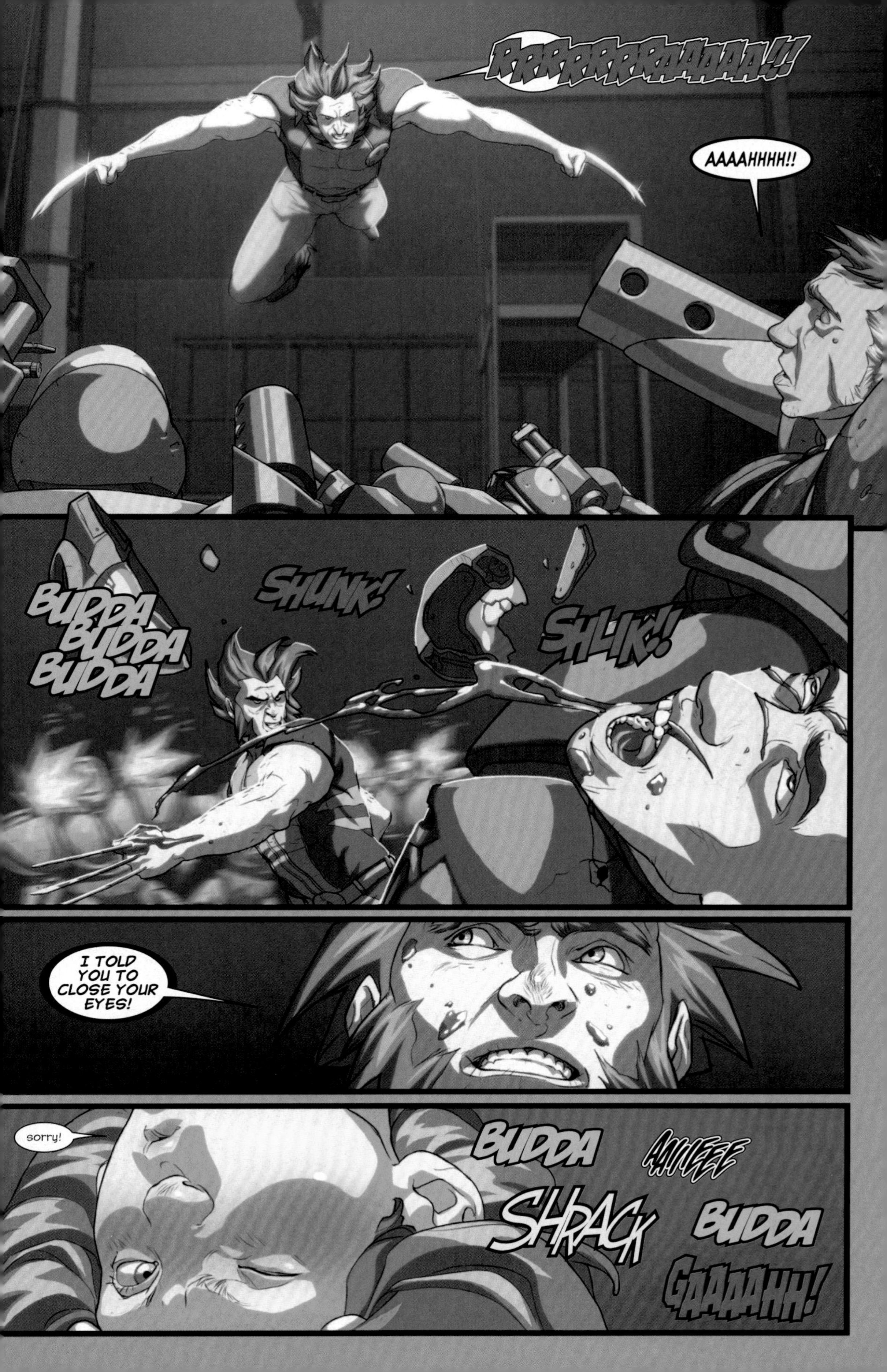
RRRRRRRRAAAAA!!
AAAAHHHH!!
BUDDA BUDDA BUDDA
SHUNK!
SHLIK!!
I TOLD YOU TO CLOSE YOUR EYES!
sorry!
BUDDA
AAIIEEE
SHRACK
BUDDA
GAAAAHH!

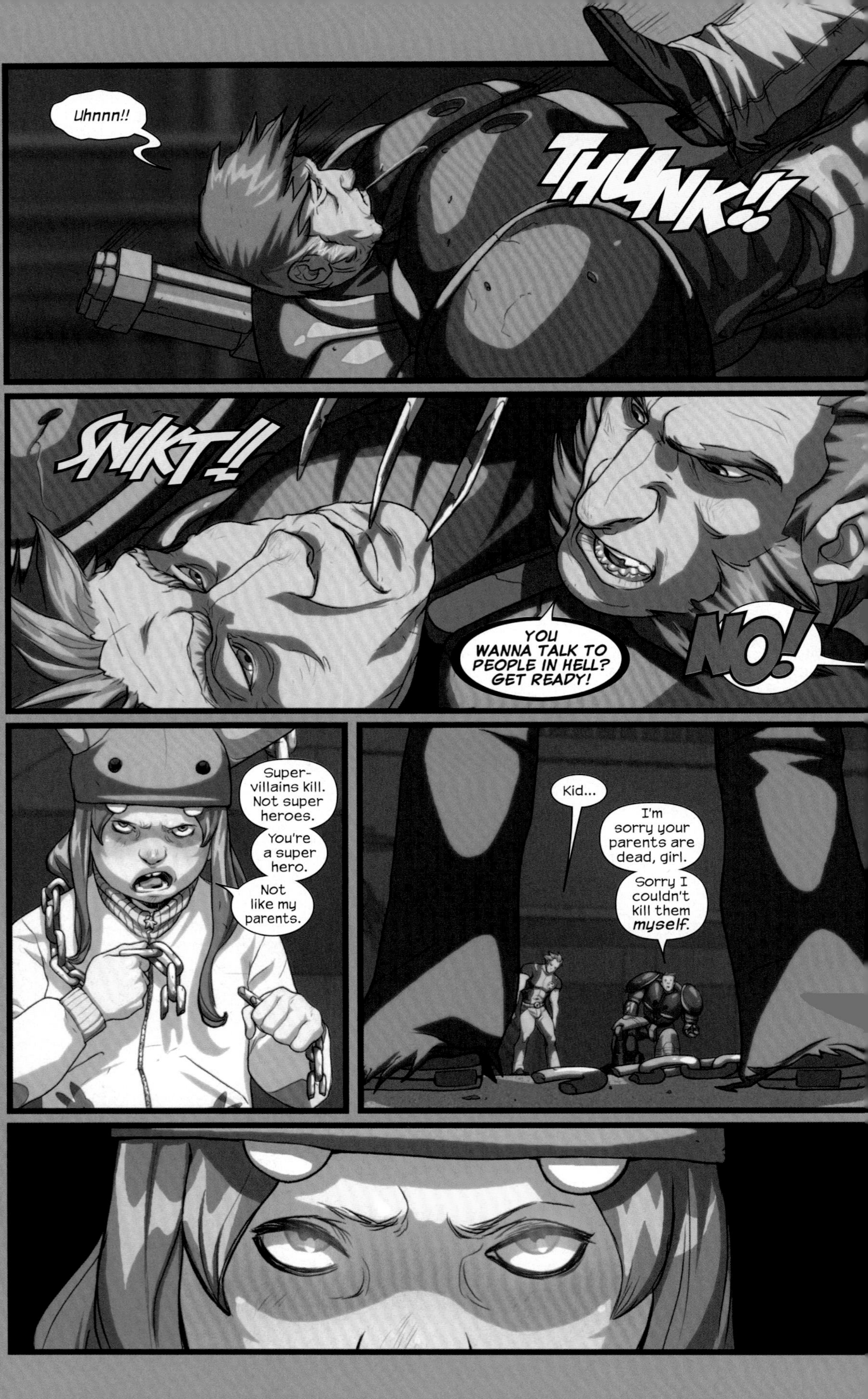
Uhnnn!!
THUNK!!
SNIKT!!
YOU WANNA TALK TO PEOPLE IN HELL? GET READY!
NO!
Super-villains kill. Not super heroes.
You're a super hero.
Not like my parents.
Kid...
I'm sorry your parents are dead, girl.
Sorry I couldn't kill them *myself*.

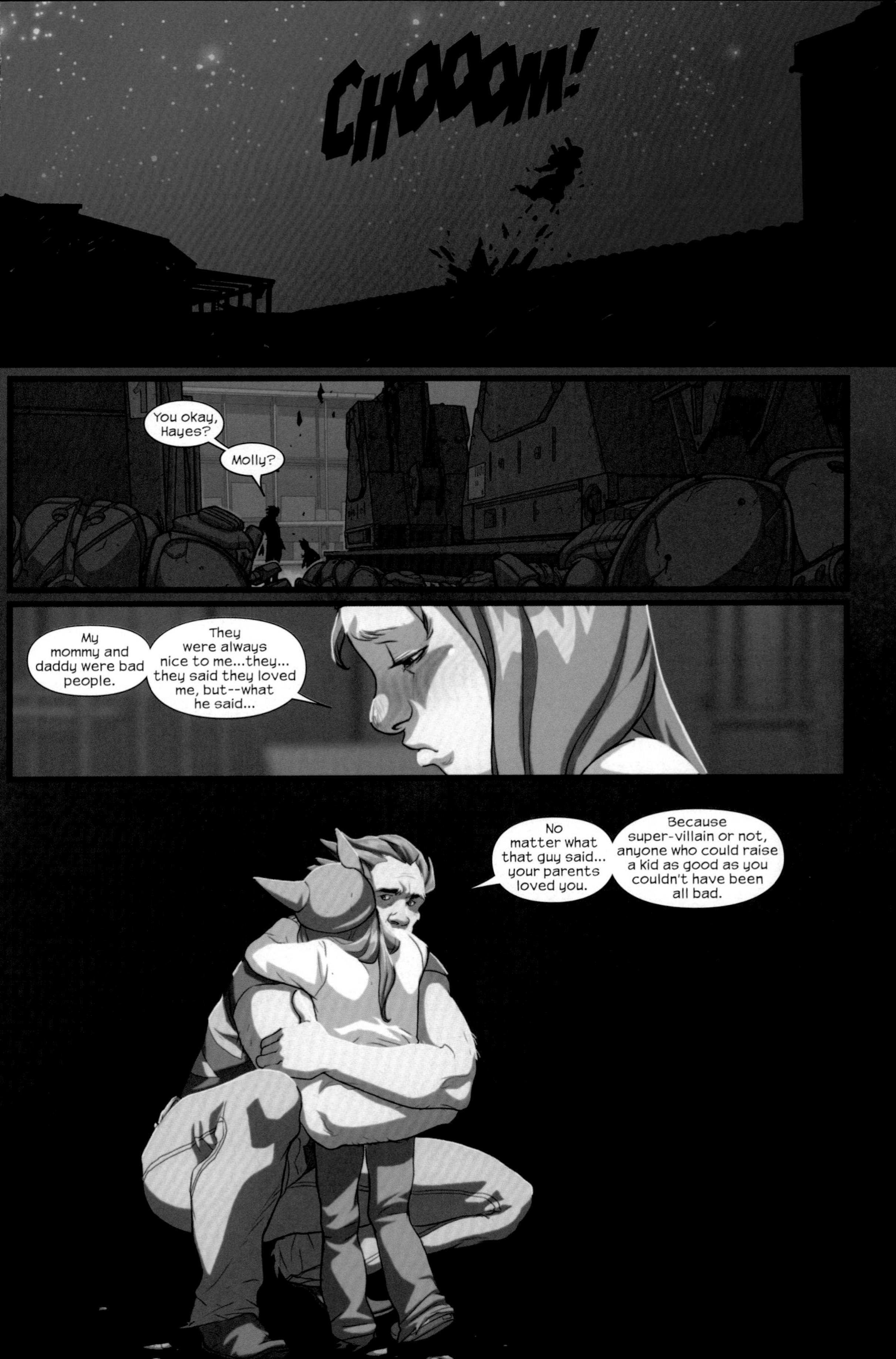
CHOOOM!
You okay, Hayes?
Molly?
My mommy and daddy were bad people.
They were always nice to me...they... they said they loved me, but--what he said...
No matter what that guy said... your parents loved you.
Because super-villain or not, anyone who could raise a kid as good as you couldn't have been all bad.

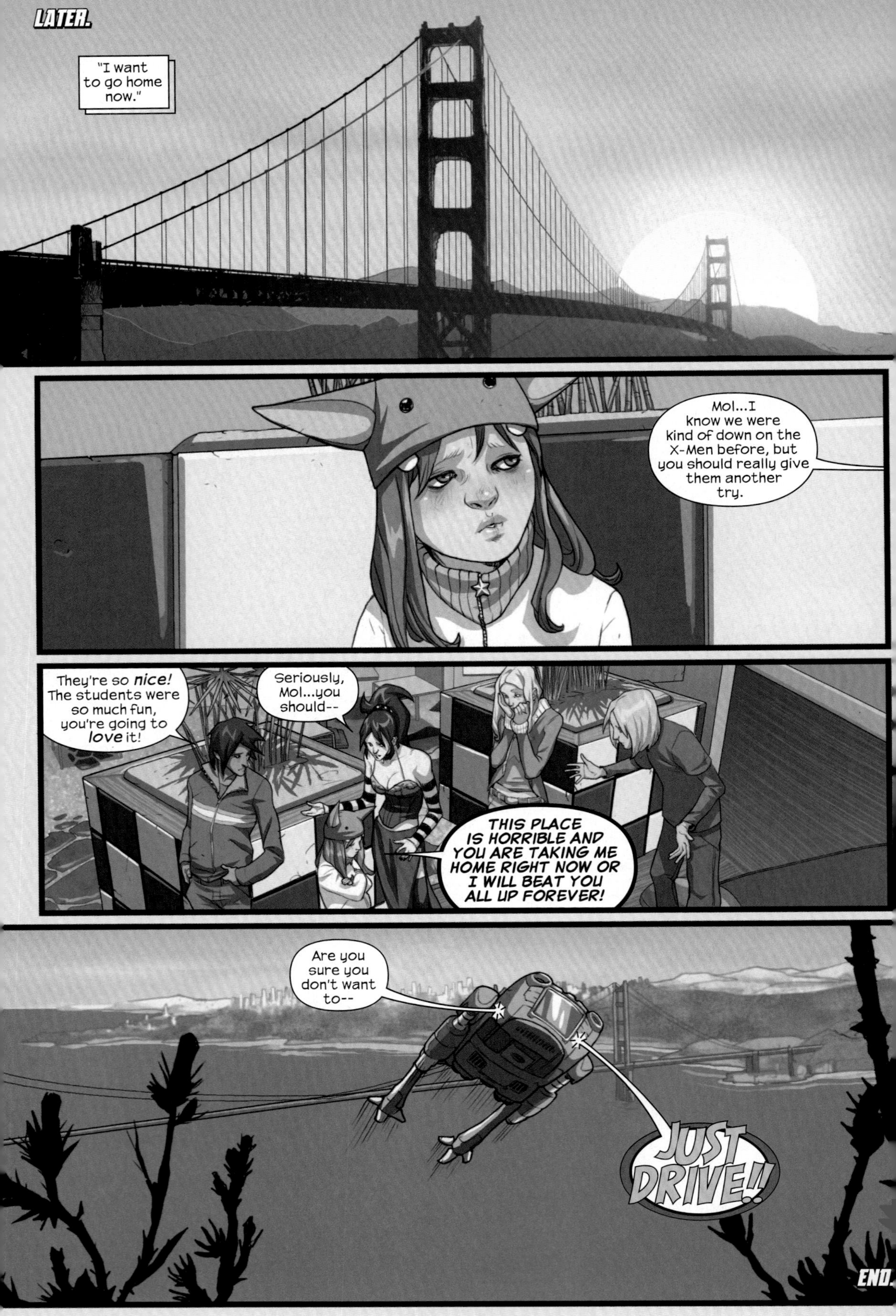
LATER.
"I want to go home now."
Mol...I know we were kind of down on the X-Men before, but you should really give them another try.
They're so *nice!* The students were so much fun, you're going to *love* it!
Seriously, Mol...you should--
THIS PLACE IS HORRIBLE AND YOU ARE TAKING ME HOME RIGHT NOW OR I WILL BEAT YOU ALL UP FOREVER!
Are you sure you don't want to--
JUST DRIVE!!
END.

So wait-- do these guys have anything to do with *Cobra*? As in "Commander"?

No. Totally different serpent commandos.

Mostly because these guys are real, and G.I. Joe is not. They're white supremacists.

So they dress up like snakes?? How does that make their point?

Are these guys complete morons or something?

They're white supremacists, Chase. So...yes.

WHOOOO-AM!

LOOK OUT!

Ahhahee ‹sniff› hee... ahh...

AGH!

Ta-daaa!

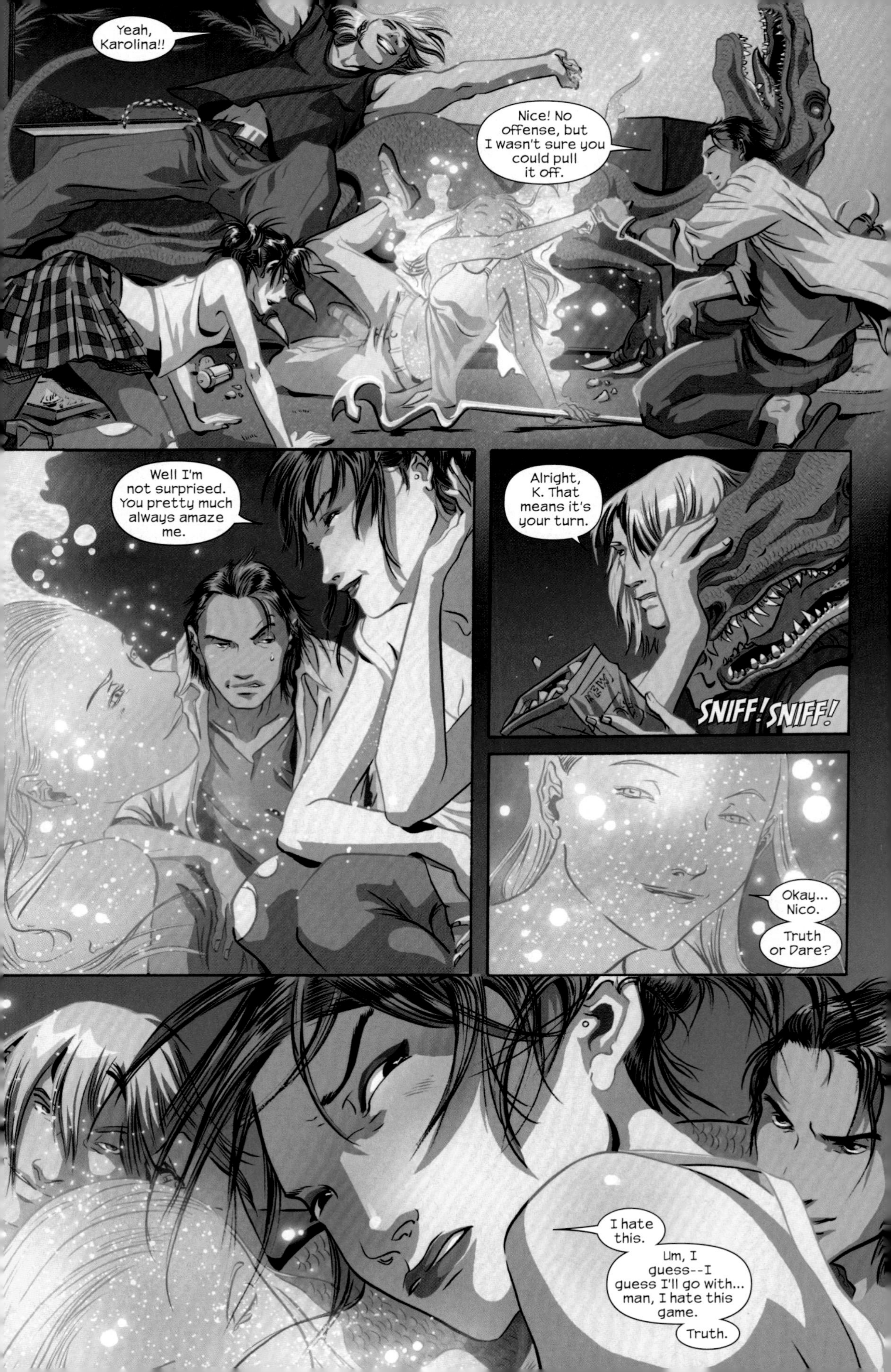

Yeah, Karolina!!
Nice! No offense, but I wasn't sure you could pull it off.
Well I'm not surprised. You pretty much always amaze me.
Alright, K. That means it's your turn.
SNIFF! SNIFF!
Okay... Nico.
Truth or Dare?
I hate this.
Um, I guess--I guess I'll go with... man, I hate this game.
Truth.

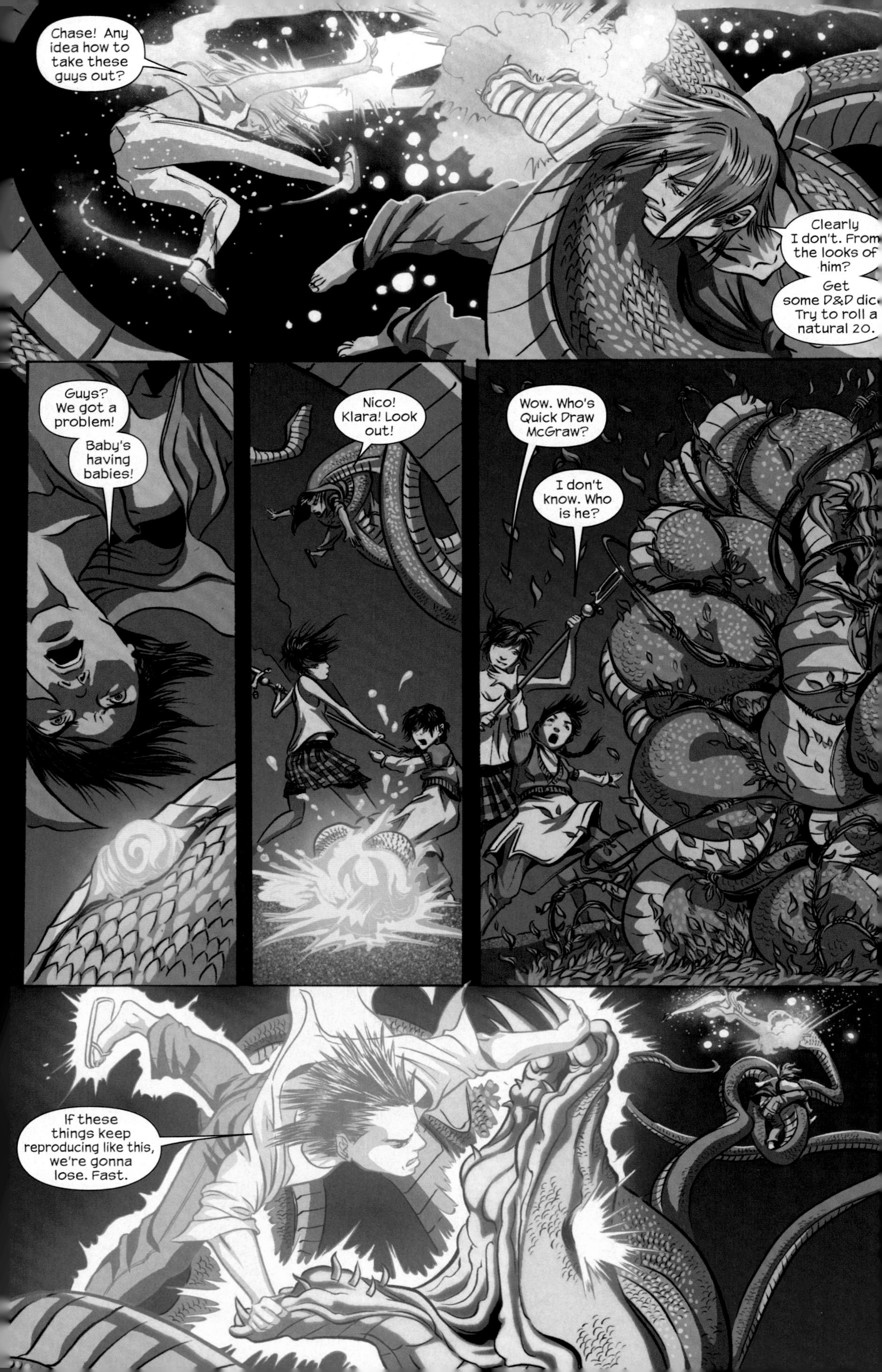
Chase! Any idea how to take these guys out?
Clearly I don't. From the looks of him?
Get some D&D dic Try to roll a natural 20.
Guys? We got a problem!
Baby's having babies!
Nico! Klara! Look out!
Wow. Who's Quick Draw McGraw?
I don't know. Who is he?
If these things keep reproducing like this, we're gonna lose. Fast.

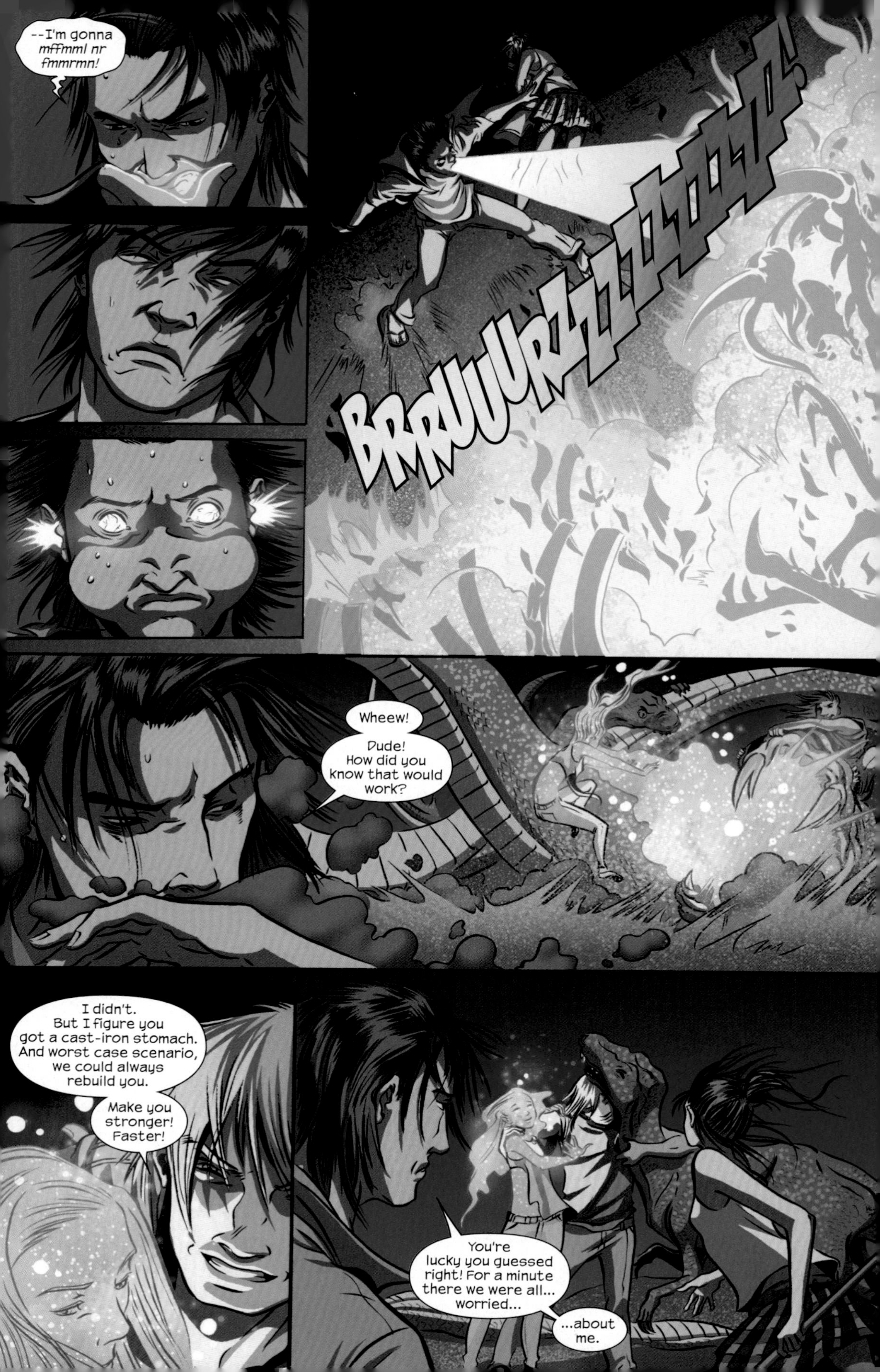

--I'm gonna mffmml nr fmmrmn!
BRRUUURZZZZZZZZZZZ!
Wheew!
Dude! How did you know that would work?
I didn't. But I figure you got a cast-iron stomach. And worst case scenario, we could always rebuild you.
Make you stronger! Faster!
You're lucky you guessed right! For a minute there we were all... worried...
...about me.

THE END.

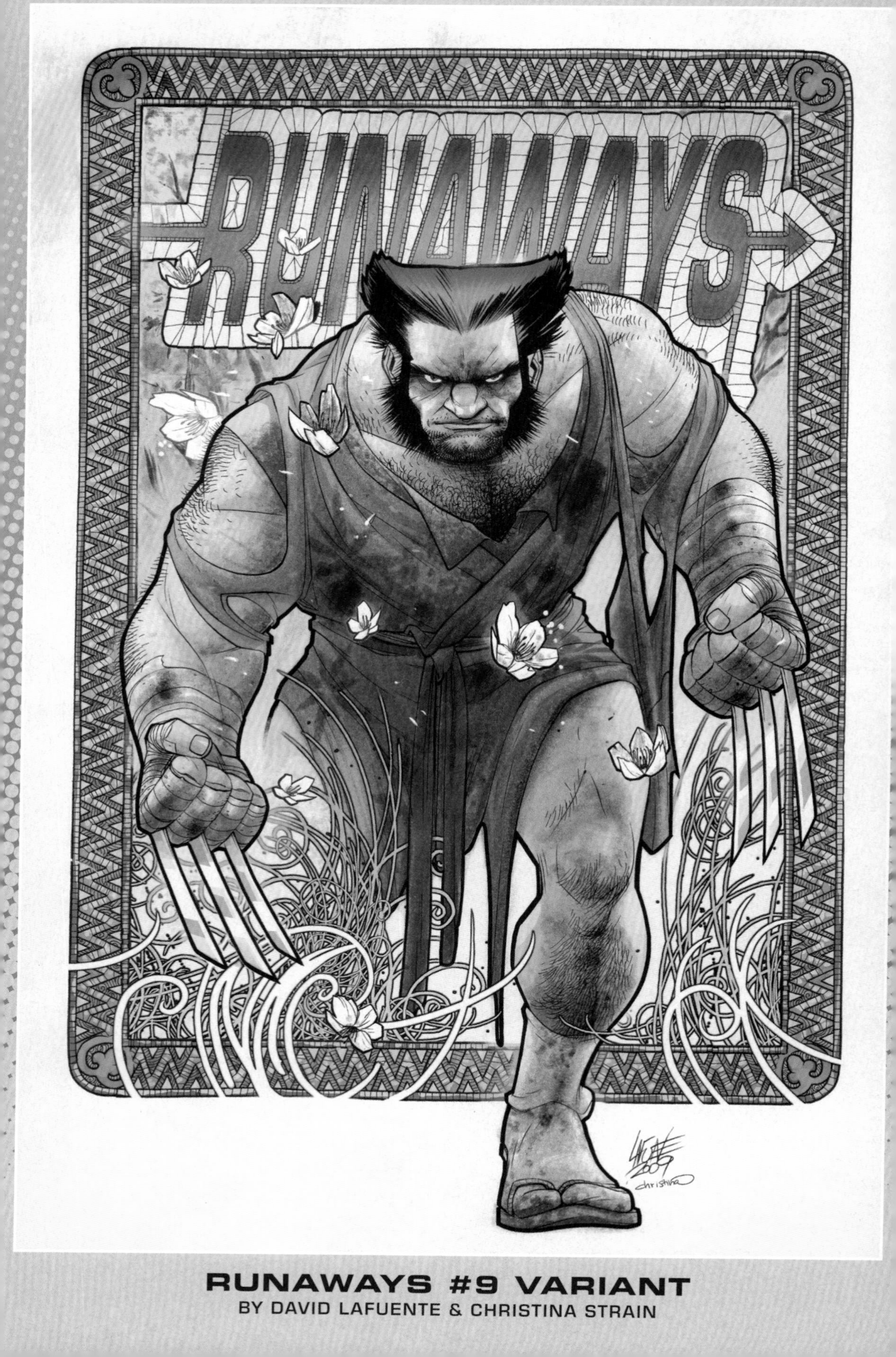
RUNAWAYS

RUNAWAYS #9 VARIANT
BY DAVID LAFUENTE & CHRISTINA STRAIN

RUNAWAYS SKETCHES

BY EMMA RIOS

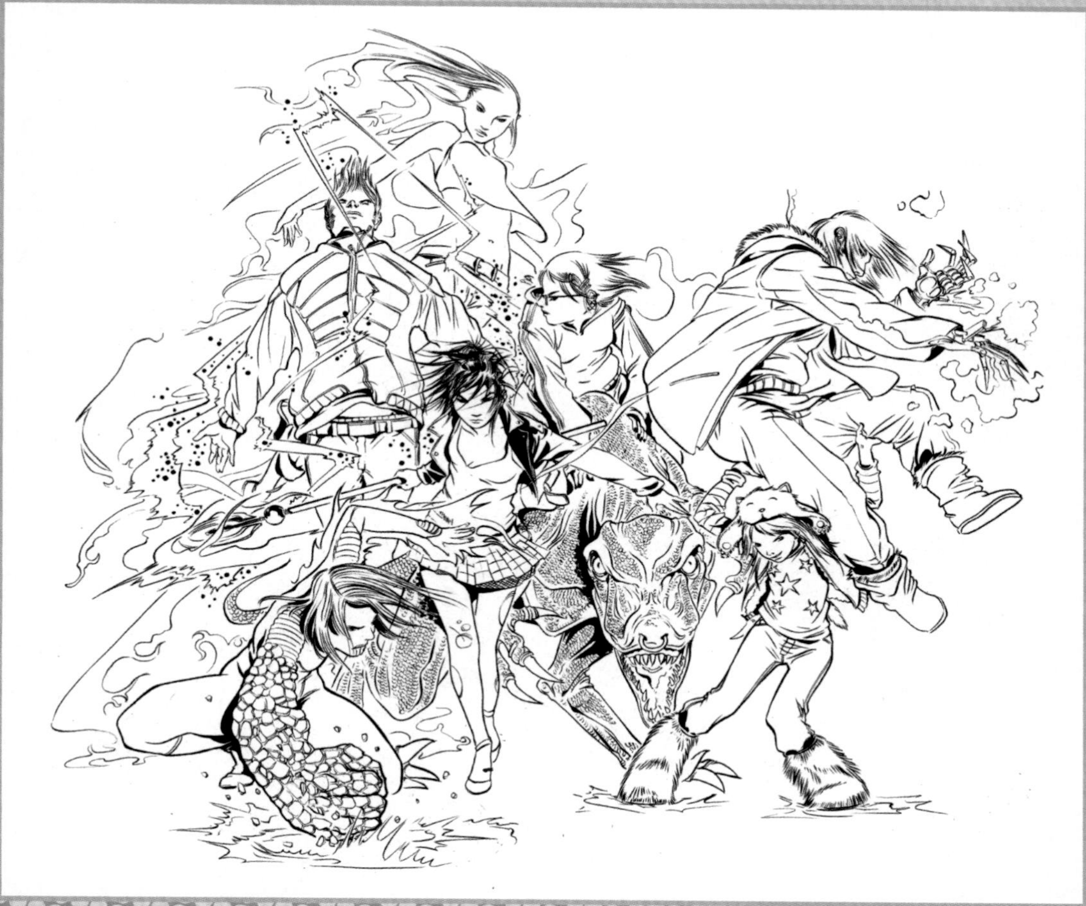

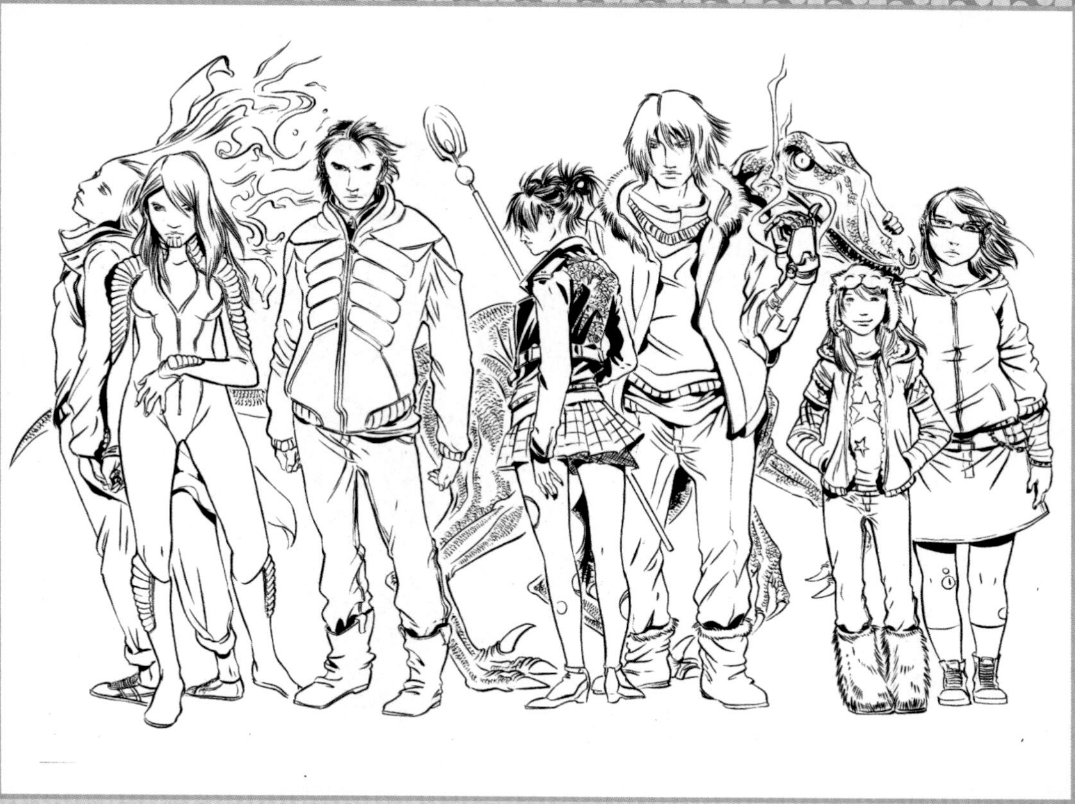

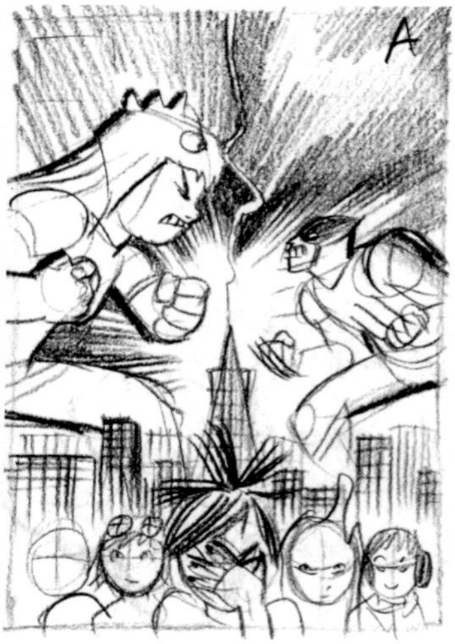
A

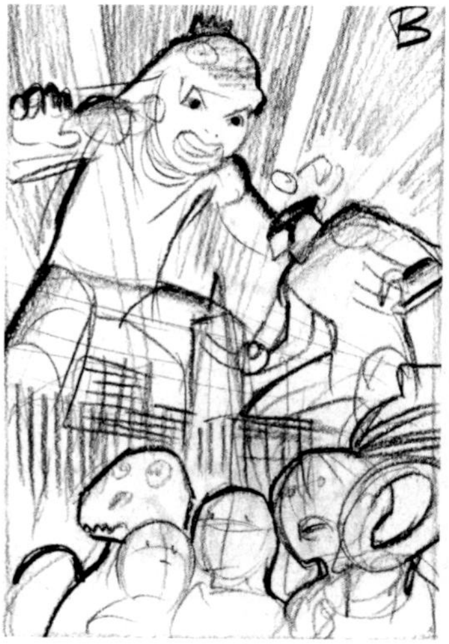
B

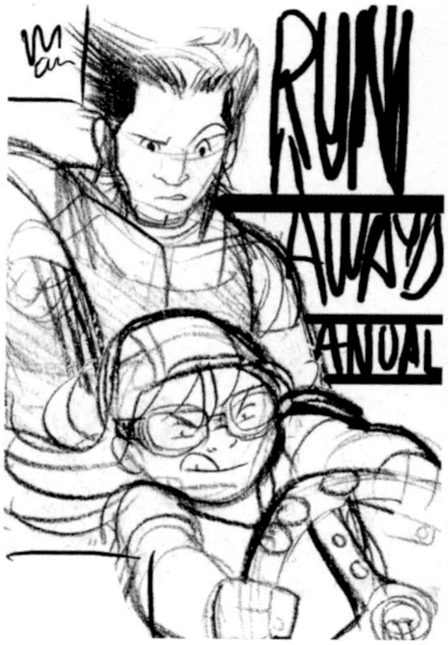
RUN
AWAYS
ANUAL

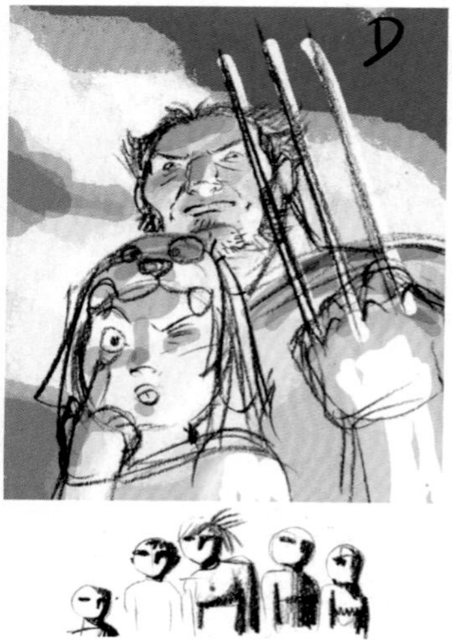
D

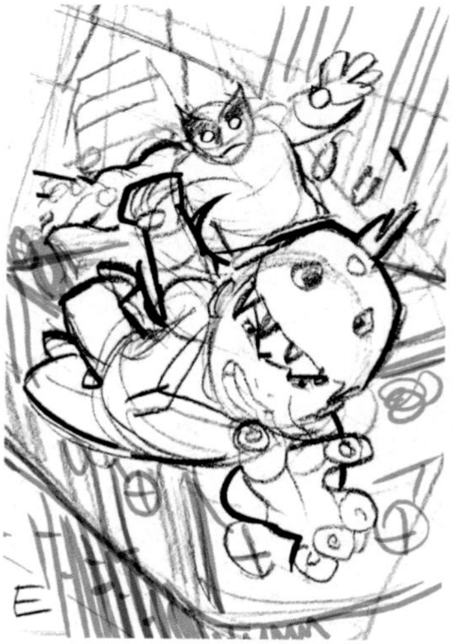
E

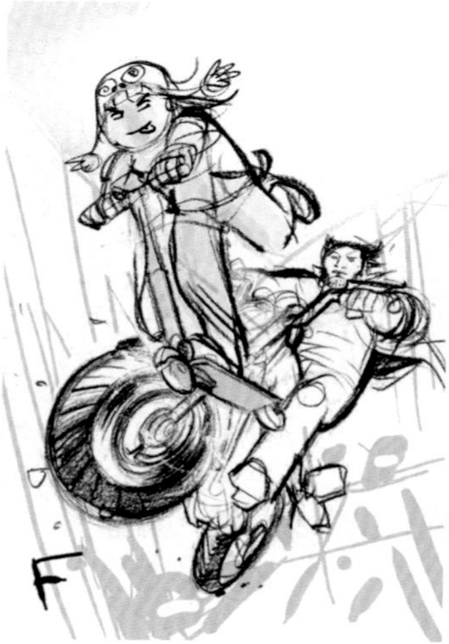
F

#10 COVER PROCESS

BY DAVID LAFUENTE
& CHRISTINA STRAIN

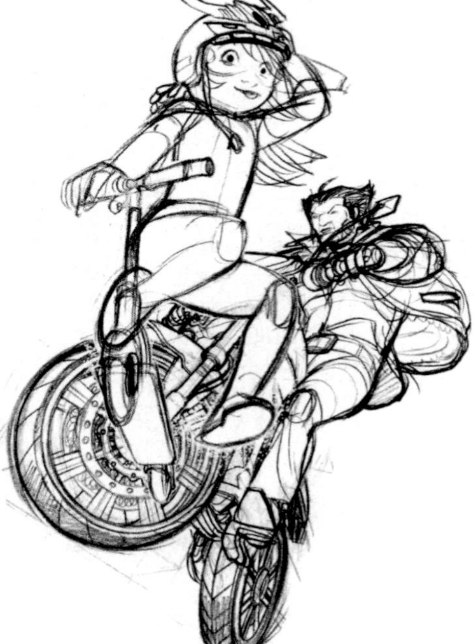

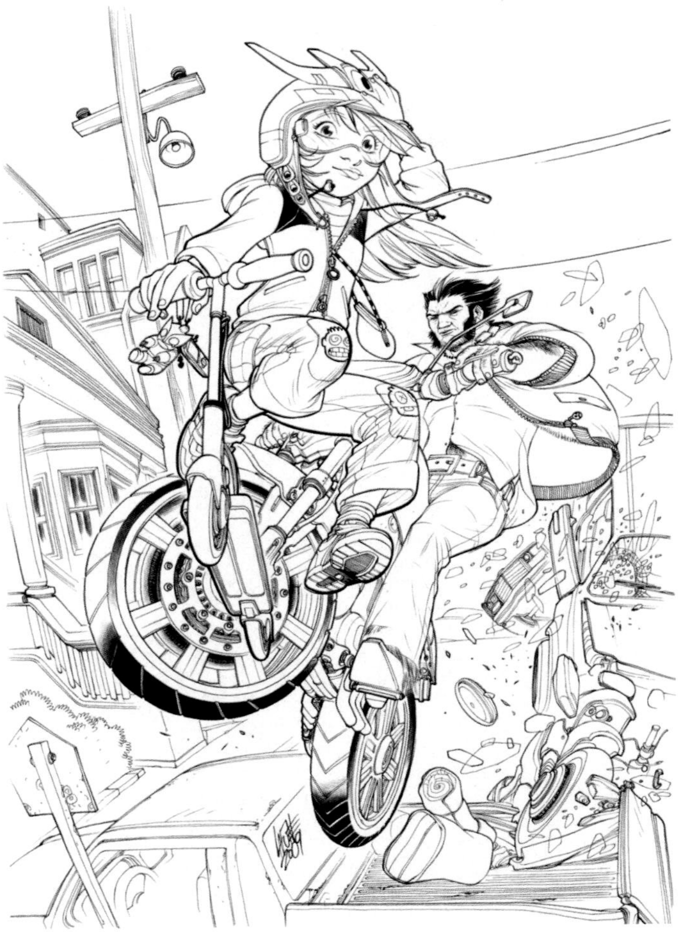

ALTERNATE COLORS

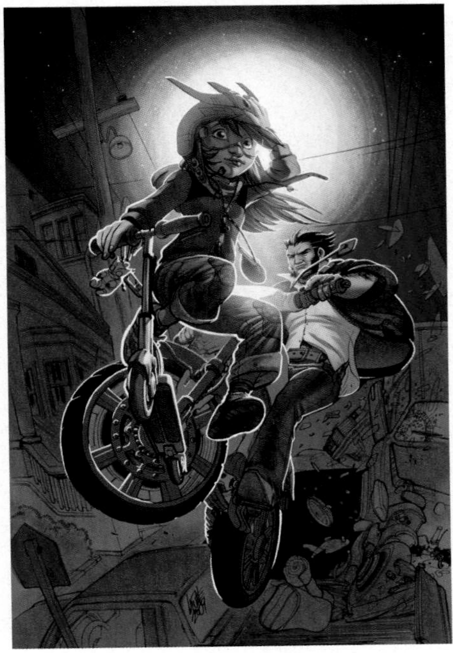

FINAL

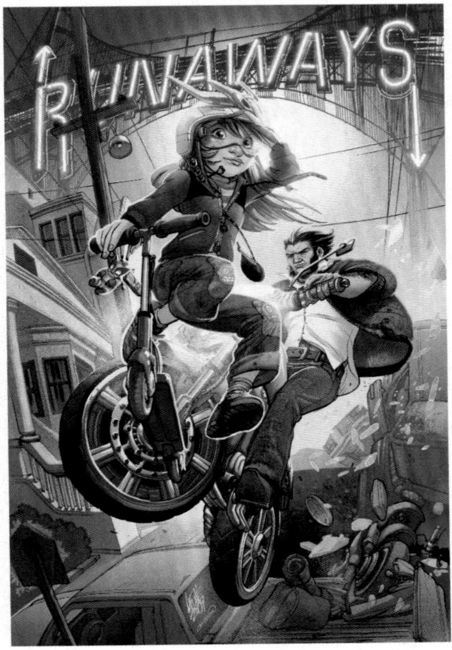
RUNAWAYS